The Four Walls *of* My Freedom

The Four Walls *of* My Freedom

Donna Thomson

ANANSI

First published in Canada in 2010 by McArthur & Company

This edition published in 2014 by
House of Anansi Press Inc.
110 Spadina Avenue, Suite 801
Toronto, ON, M5V 2K4
Tel. 416-363-4343 • Fax 416-363-1017
www.houseofanansi.com

Distributed in Canada by
HarperCollins Canada Ltd.
1995 Markham Road
Scarborough, ON, M1B 5M8
Toll free tel. 1-800-387-0117

Distributed in the United States by
Publishers Group West
1700 Fourth Street
Berkeley, CA 94710
Toll free tel. 1-800-788-3123

Permission is gratefully acknowledged to reprint the following:

"You'll Never Walk Alone" by Richard Rodgers & Oscar Hammerstein II © 1945 Williamson Music.
Copyright renewed. International copyright secured. All rights reserved.
Used by permission of Williamson Music, a division of The Rodgers & Hammerstein Organization,
an Imagem Company.

"Welcome to Holland" © Emily Perl Kingsley is reprinted by kind permission of the author.

The Idea of Justice by Amartya Sen, Cambridge, Mass.: The Belknap Press of Harvard University
Press. Copyright © 2009 Amartya Sen.

House of Anansi Press is committed to protecting our natural environment.
As part of our efforts, the interior of this book is printed on paper that contains 100%
post-consumer recycled fibres, is acid-free, and is processed chlorine-free.

18 17 16 15 14   1 2 3 4 5

Library and Archives Canada Cataloguing in Publication

Thomson, Donna, 1955–, author
The four walls of my freedom / Donna Thomson.

Issued in print and electronic formats.
ISBN 978-1-77089-479-2 (pbk.). ISBN 978-1-77089-480-8 (epub).

1. Thomson, Donna, 1955–. 2. Thomson, Donna, 1955– —Family. 3. Mothers of children
with disabilities—Canada—Biography. 4. Cerebral palsy—Family relationships—Canada.
5. Cerebral palsy—Canada—Biography. I. Title.

HQ759.913.T482 2014   649'.151   C2013-906986-0   C2013-906987-9

Library of Congress Control Number: 2013918883

Cover design: Alysia Shewchuk (adapted from the hardcover by Tania Craan)
Text design and typesetting: McArthur & Company

Canada Council   Conseil des Arts   ONTARIO ARTS COUNCIL
for the Arts   du Canada   CONSEIL DES ARTS DE L'ONTARIO

*We acknowledge for their financial support of our publishing program the Canada Council for the Arts,
the Ontario Arts Council, and the Government of Canada through the Canada Book Fund.*

Printed and bound in Canada

RECYCLED
Paper made from
recycled material
FSC® C103567
www.fsc.org

To my family

CONTENTS

This is a book that had to be written. It had to be written for two reasons. The first is to explain the world of people with disabilities. They have rights and needs that must be looked at by all of us from a philosophical view and a policy point of view. Secondly, this book had to be written because it tells the story of Nicholas and his family, Donna, Jim, and Natalie. This story needed to be told for Nicholas' sake. He has something to say to us, as does his family.

It is essential to put these two things together — the ideas surrounding the world of disabilities and the reality lived by those with disabilities and their families. It all makes sense if these two elements are put together. It makes sense because it forces us to realize that Nicholas is a citizen with citizen's rights, and none of the services he receives are the result of the kindness of the rest of us. The services he should and must receive have nothing to do with charity. They should come to him as any service comes to a citizen. And that is as it should be in a fully functioning civilization where we make the effort to imagine *the Other*. Donna Thomson has done a wonderful job at blending these two themes together. And so *The Four Walls of My Freedom* is an eloquent expression of both personal lives and public philosophy.

I first met Donna at Government House in Ottawa a decade ago. We talked about her involvement with PLAN, a wonderful organization that has developed whole new approaches towards the linking of citizenship and people with disabilities. She asked me if I would become the Patron of PLAN and I immediately agreed. The simplest explanation for my enthusiasm is that my brother Anthony had disabilities. And he had them at a time when Canada had virtually no decent public services for him. Canada treated the whole question of disabilities as one of charity. He was a wonderful brother. And my mother, like mothers almost everywhere, had to fight the system to ensure that he was treated properly — as a citizen. We have come a long way in Canada and in other democracies when it comes to disabilities. Our civilization has evolved in the right direction. But Donna's story is a reminder that we have not gone far enough and we certainly haven't gone fast enough.

I think what she brings to the table is a very clear evocation of the contributions that people with disabilities make to our society. They want to make every contribution they can. And they have to make a greater effort than most people in order to carry out those contributions. That energy and courage and consciousness of people with disabilities carries a strong lesson for their fellow citizens who, quite frankly, have an easy time of it in comparison.

One of the themes that keeps coming through in Donna's writing is that every time a circle is created to ensure that there are contacts and friendship around a person with disabilities, the people who join the circle quickly realize that they are the primary beneficiaries.

This is a moving book, in part because it is about Nicholas, but also because it is about all of us and our capacity to live together. If we can embrace the citizenship of people with disabilities, then we will all learn how to live together.

John Ralston Saul
Toronto, July 2010

CHAPTER ONE

The Beginning

The baby book said to rock a crying infant at the same rate as a mother's heart rate. Anywhere between 60 and 100 beats per minute it said. I split the difference and tried 80 beats per minute which is VERY fast, if you have never tried it. Not rocking really, just an oscillating pressure on the ball of one foot if one's legs are crossed.

But my baby son kept crying and crying, once for thirty-seven hours in a row. His back arched, his high-pitched catlike screams would pierce the night. I rocked and sang Christmas carols to the time of 80 beats per minute. Keeping my arms relaxed was tricky. I thought if I could just relax the arms that held him, my baby would sink limply and quietly into sleep.

"Who knows what makes the little turkeys cry?" mused the doctor a little too quickly when I reported that perhaps my baby was crying much more than he should. "Change the formula." At a new mother's group, I noticed that other babies weren't screaming. There was coffee on offer and I took a muffin as well. Nick screeched, arched his back and the coffee spilt, the muffin broke on the floor.

The group leader stared in horror and all the mothers and babies blinked in alarm. "We don't belong here," I thought, and ran out, leaving the mess on the floor. After that, I kept indoors. The blinds were closed because light seemed to infuriate Nicholas. We kept our voices to whispers because an exclamation or laugh caused his arms and legs to flail outwards suddenly, setting off some horror only he knew. I kept him swaddled so he wouldn't feel like his legs and arms would fly off his body in these moments of panic.

I couldn't persuade Nicholas' mouth into an effective suck. Why couldn't he swallow without choking? His nappy remained dry for a day and the baby book said "take him to the hospital." The check-in clerk in Emergency at the Ottawa Children's Hospital asked Nick's age. "One month," I replied. My turn to choke.

The white-haired doctor stooped to look closely at Nicholas and asked, "Has anyone spoken to you about your son's development?"

"No," I answered, "he is small because he was a bit premature at thirty-three weeks. Someone crashed into the back of my car at twenty-six weeks and they think that's why he was born early." Only later I learned that "development" meant cerebral palsy or mental retardation.

Three months later, Nicholas was admitted to hospital so that tests could be performed. The doctor asked me if I would like to hear the results. I nodded. She closed the ward playroom door for privacy. We were alone. She, in her lab coat, was sitting in a sturdy mother's wooden rocker. I was squeezed into a plastic child's chair. Around us lay discarded toys and empty chunky bright tables and chairs, all toddler-sized. Tears glistened on the doctor's cheeks as she told me my baby was severely disabled. "Never be normal" are the words I remember. I also remember "generalized cerebral atrophy." Pea brain, I wondered?

"Esophageal reflux," she said. "Nothing to keep food down where it belongs. Common in cerebral palsy. Pain similar to heart attack." There were blue stripes on her blouse. I looked down and something red caught my eye. Blood was oozing from the edge of my thumbnail where I had bitten it. "Well, I'm in the right place," I thought.

I stood up and felt a lightness, a sense of relief and purpose. "Now I will be able to feed my child," I thought. "I will become an expert. I will apply myself to becoming a great mother, and my baby will grow into someone perfectly perfect." Passing the desk, I noticed the nurses half turned, whispering, their pitying eyes fixed on us. I scooped up Nicholas, deposited him into a pram and paraded up and down the hospital halls, back straight, eyes fixed directly ahead. But I was not all right. I wrote in our baby book: "February 22–25, 1989: Nick admitted to hospital. Cat scan, PH probe and digestive barium x-rays all abnormal — we trying [sic] to absorb this terrible news."

I remember hearing a radio news report a long time ago about a terrible road accident in rural England. A young family — parents and three children — had all perished. The grandfather's public response was, "I don't understand — we brought them up so carefully so nothing like this would ever happen." I felt like this grandfather — the experience of falling victim to random tragedy and a serious derailment of one's life plans caused such profound shock and questioning of all I believed was solid and true.

At that time, my husband, Jim, was on loan from Foreign Affairs to the Prime Minister's Office and would come home near bedtime, still suited, to feed Nicholas while watching the news. Word spread in our family about the "condition." A cousin came over with a friend to give advice. The friend's business card read "Volunteer Consultant to Families with a Child with a Disability." Her name was Kathleen Jordan and she had a son of sixteen with incomprehensible difficulties. He was blind, had cerebral palsy, Tourette syndrome and epilepsy. I started to examine this blonde woman in my living room. Her nails were beautiful, glossy red and perfectly rounded. I asked, "How is it you have time to do your nails?" I really wanted to know.

Kathleen had a huge pile of papers with her. She patted me and said, "I have some information here, but I completely understand if you want to look at it some other time." "No!" I cried, "Give them to me now! All of it." Years later, I heard the expression "cognitive lifeboat." In that moment, I found mine, and, gasping, climbed aboard.

Sometimes, words on a page leap out and punch you in the face. Wake up! This is what you need to know! In that pile of paper was a story about something called "Conductive Education." First of all, I like the word *education*. It suggests a capacity for learning. It suggests power and control through knowledge.

Andras Peto was a Hungarian and a practical innovator. He looked at the state education system of his country, saw that walking was a prerequisite of accessing the national curriculum, looked at the thousands of bright children who did not walk because of disability and decided to think of a way around the problem. Peto devised a system of teaching children with cerebral palsy and adults who had had a stroke how to control their own bodies. He believed that each functional, bodily movement could be broken down into smaller movements that could be taught and practised, using rhythm as the primary teaching tool. People with no functional movement could be taught to brush their own teeth, sit independently, and even walk through the school doors. This was an approach that required hope and determination. "Right," I thought, "this is for us."

A speech therapist advised that Nicholas could suck and swallow if he was fed sitting upright. I had discovered Conductive Education. Nicholas smiled. The screaming continued, but in between, oh the power of those smiles! I nicknamed him "Bunnybear" as a nod to his Jekyll and Hyde personality. For his first birthday, I made two cakes: one a bunny, the other a bear. Jim and I drank champagne and congratulated ourselves on surviving.

The local treatment centre for children with disabilities made us sign a paper promising not to pursue alternative therapies. I signed. Then I hired a private Conductive Education specialist, Rosalind, who had trained in England, and came for our first home appointment. "Look at the window, look at the door. Look at the ceiling, look at the floor," she sang as she held Nicholas on her knee. My mother was visiting. As Rosalind sang, Nicholas looked around, up and down. My mother clapped her hands. Nicholas startled, screamed, and I hugged Rosalind.

Another woman called Barbara came to our house once a week to help me teach Nicholas something called infant stimulation. She suggested that I use a photo album with large magazine pictures or photographs of things he knew something about — things like "Mum," "dog," "flower." Barbara walked with me to the park down the street on a sunny, warm day. She instructed me to let Nicholas lie in the grass on his back and then gently turn him on his side. His mouth opened and he began to chew on several blades of grass. "Terrific!" Barbara proclaimed. "Now let's do some tree bark." She reassured me that none of these natural items could kill Nick and encouraged me to make the most of our dog Amanda in the stimulation regime. Amanda was a golden retriever with a strong mothering instinct — sometimes, I thought, stronger than mine. Nicholas would lie on a blanket on the floor with Amanda lying alongside, her head resting on his belly. Nicholas would open and close his tiny fists in her fur and suddenly, fist clenched, he would pull hard, unable to let go. Amanda would simply turn to look at this spot on her back where a clump of fur was being yanked with appalling strength. Then her mouth would reach his fist. She licked his fist until it relaxed and opened. She would jump up and run to me, tail wagging, eyes watery. She would bury her head between my legs and I'd say, "I'm sorry, darling. But you are such a good mum to Nick, so gentle. Good girl."

"You should write a book," people said. No, I thought, why should anyone care about a family such as ours? We are so different, such an aberration. Like anyone who has tried to protect the integrity of a loved one with a nasty chronic condition, my life with Nicholas has been infused with a desperate love. There have been days with lots of laughter, but there have also been days when Nick was in terrible pain or was unable to eat or drink, his stomach angrily rejecting its role as a digestive organ.

What happened to him? Why is he like that? Did you smoke? Did you drink? How about the hair dye you used? Maybe you were too old to have babies. It must have been something you did. He's underweight. What are you feeding him? Can't you feed him more? Can't you stop him arching backwards like that? Don't let him roll over in that position. I know that mothers with their first babies can feel incompetent and sometimes depressed. I felt assaulted by fear. I knew for a fact that every professional was judging me, every relative, every neighbour. Maybe even God was judging me.

When Nicholas was about one year old, I decided to have him baptized. Brought up as a Catholic, I had not been to church in years. Jim is an Anglican who spent his Sunday mornings immersed in newspapers, coffee in hand. I have often thought of my Catholic roots as like those of my grey hair. No matter how much dye you apply, those roots keep growing back. I worried about Nicholas dying before being baptized. I had read that the Church had officially discarded Limbo as a concept, but what if they were wrong? I found a nearby Catholic church in the Yellow Pages and made an appointment for a home visit with the priest. I nervously set out the tea with favourite cups belonging to my grandmother. A distinguished, outdoorsy-looking gentleman with a thick shock of steely grey hair and wearing all-weather gear arrived at my door. I ushered Father Laurie in and explained the lapse in my lapsed Catholic status. Feeling childish, guilty and frightened, I asked him if he would baptize Nicholas. He took the porcelain blue and white cup in his large, sunburnt hand and lifted it to take a sip of tea. The saucer, stuck with sugary tea to the cup, suddenly clattered on to the glass tabletop and shattered. Father Laurie swept up the broken pieces with his hands as he promised to christen Nick. I might be condemned, but Nicholas would be redeemed.

On June 11, 1989, Nicholas was baptized. The mass that day had a children's choir marching down the centre aisle singing and waving a banner that read "We all belong."

"Hmmm," I realized, "I love this! They CAN'T kick us out!" I circulated a celebratory photograph to the family showing Nicholas munching on the baptismal order of service. I called it "Nicholas trying to digest organized religion."

By that time, Nick and I were already regulars at the local rehabilitation centre where we attended physio, occupational and speech therapies every week. The speech therapist was a kind, enthusiastic woman from New Jersey.

I joked with her that when Nicholas learned to talk, he'd be taken for a Yank. In her small white room, she placed a doll on Nick's wheelchair tray and asked him to choose a piece of clothing for her to wear. Nick stared at the ceiling. She asked me if I was using bubbles with him at home. "Bubbles?" I asked. "Um, no. Sorry."

"Well, you should definitely be using bubbles. Children like Nicholas need practice visually tracking a moving object. And when he reaches to pop bubbles that are in front of his face, he will be reaching toward the midline of his body — something that is naturally very difficult for him to do. You must have noticed that his arms are usually bent by his head and arching backwards." I lowered my eyes and nodded silently.

I drove home, stopping to buy a plastic jar of bubbles with its potent life-changing possibilities. I blew the whole jar at Nick when we got home and we giggled as they popped.

In the mail, I received a letter inviting me and Jim to a meeting of Nick's team at the rehab centre. They would discuss his progress in therapy and announce to us their results of his cognition testing. They would recommend a preschool placement. Nicholas was just over a year old at the time.

I had begun to understand that meetings about Nicholas took place amongst professionals without me or Jim there. Jim and I arrived an hour early for our "team" meeting. I managed to locate our social worker and in urgent whispers pleaded with her to allow us into ALL discussions about

Nicholas. I was afraid of them talking and deciding my son's fate without us. I had reason to be afraid.

There was a fish tank in the waiting room and other families waited quietly with us. Some children were much older and sat in elaborate wheelchairs, heads turned, teeth crooked. I still wasn't quite used to such differences, but I wasn't staring. I felt anxious and breathless in this atmosphere of inertia. I scanned the hallway behind me for activity of familiar faces; I tried to peer into the boardroom window to see if our "team" was meeting without me. Lynn, our social worker, finally swept around the corner and apologized for the delay in proceedings. She ushered Jim and me into the boardroom to greet seven frozen half-smiles. Something felt terribly wrong. Each therapist was asked to review Nick's progress or lack of it and I noticed that Lynn was concentrating on her notes. Everything they said seemed to be truthful enough until: "We find that Nicholas is profoundly delayed. We recommend that he goes to a preschool operated by the Ottawa District Association for the Mentally Retarded."

I looked around the room. There were two doors, one leading back into the waiting room and another leading to a hallway on the opposite side. So they had already conducted Nicholas' case conference without me and Jim. At the end of their private meeting, Lynn had walked out the back door of the boardroom, around the corner to the waiting room and now she wasn't looking me. I felt my face hot, it was hard to swallow. "I am one of you!" I shouted silently. "I am on this team!" I shook some nonexistent stray lock of hair off my forehead, breathed deeply into my nostrils and began. "Nicholas is a very bright boy, exceptionally bright, in fact." The occupational therapist, head tilted and looking miserable and desperately sad, whispered, "Is there an example of that you can tell us about?" I was beaten, cheated and I knew it.

We went to have a look at the brand-new Cumberland Hub Preschool about half an hour outside Ottawa. Moira was the petite, gentle, redheaded director who greeted us. Nick's classmates would be other children with severe physical and mental disabilities. There was a boisterous gang of children with Down syndrome, but they were kept separate from our little group. Nick's classroom was sunny, warm and quiet, except for some soft classical music playing in the background. Moira exuded reassurance, competence and kindness. I knew that destiny had nudged me through these doors and I knew it was the best place for my baby son who still couldn't manage any kind of sudden noise. Still, I knew he wasn't mentally challenged and I resolved to defend his intellect at all costs.

In times of trouble, my principal survival tool is my telephone. Around the time of Nicholas' diagnosis, I rifled through the Yellow Pages searching for information and assistance for our family. I had telephoned every listing under Associations, Societies, Institutes and Foundations. I even rang up the Opimian Society and made a note of their number when I was told it was a club for wine lovers. I might need it some day! Who knew what the future held? But when I discovered the Easter Seals Society, I realized that I had struck gold.

They sponsored a Parent Participation group that held

regional as well as provincial conferences for families to exchange experiences and information about their children who had physical disabilities. Here, one could advocate for political change. In those days, Easter Seals had money to fly us out of town for the province-wide conferences. I was severely sleep-deprived and emotionally exhausted, but as I chatted with other parents, my hunger for sharing and listening overcame all bodily concerns. I explained to another Ottawa mum how Nicholas screamed during the night.

"My daughter Carey did that until she had a surgery to correct reflux," she said. I was riveted. I knew that Nicholas had this self-same diagnosis of esophageal reflux and that he spat up many times every day. It never occurred to me, though, that all the sour milk on my shoulders could be the cause of his nightime distress.

"There's a young doctor at the hospital who did a study on this new surgery and how it can help our kids. Yes, and when they opened my Carey up, they told me she was full of it, just full of it!" Years later, I wondered what exactly the surgeons had found in Carey's chest. In that tidal wave of hopefulness, I had forgotten to ask.

The young, bespectacled doctor greeted us earnestly. As he began to explain his understanding of digestive difficulties, he crackled with the enthusiasm of a science fair prizewinner. I told the doctor Nicholas' story and he inquired about Nick's spit-up habits. On cue, I felt a familiar warm ooze on my shoulder. "Oh, I think we have a perfect candidate for this procedure right here!" he declared. I remember feeling so optimistic. I remember thinking that modern medicine and the power of love could "beat" the effects of cerebral palsy. How wrong I was.

While Nicholas was in surgery, Jim and I passed the hours in the surgical waiting room. Time dragged on and, finally, we decided to wait near Nick's bed on the ward. Another hour passed and I asked the nurse in charge if she could find out when Nicholas would be back with us. It was dusk now and she said that Nicholas was in recovery, but was "breath holding" so they were keeping him a little longer to monitor the situation. Twenty minutes later, a nurse and an orderly appeared down the hall wheeling a cot towards us. Inside was Nick, his mouth open and rigid, eyes wide with panic. He gasped, writhing, and exhaled a hoarse cry. He was in the room now, and we hovered like birds, flapping uselessly.

That night was the first, but not the last, time that I saw in my son's eyes a terrible pleading. I turned away and put my hand down on the corner chair to support myself from falling. Jim warned, "Donna, you can't do this. Come here!" I came back to Nicholas, murmuring apologies through tears. A nurse showed us how to hold the oxygen mask over Nick's face and at first he did calm down a little. The surgical resident stopped outside the door to glance at the chart and strode in. He was short with thick, black curly hair and a great deal of self-confidence. He made some inquiries about Nick's breath holding and left the room. Moments later, an awful spasm gripped Nick and we again struggled to help him breathe and relax his tiny body. His chest was bandaged where they had cut from sternum to navel and then opened his rib cage. They had inserted a feeding tube to the left of the scar that protruded like a rubber asp. It's a Foley catheter, they explained, the same as ones used for urinary purposes. It seemed huge and was sticky to the touch, an awful pseudoflesh colour. Nicholas was desperate by now, in a cycle of pain and spasm. I shouted for the nurse to help and she confided quietly that in her ten years of nursing, she had never seen a child in so much pain. As she whispered to me, the young doctor who had recommended the surgery walked in, registered the fear in our room and turned on the lights. He examined Nicholas, asked some questions about Nick's breath holding and told us that he was transferring our boy to intensive care immediately.

As we hurriedly packed up Nick's things, his babysitter came through the door, smiling and holding the string of a huge happy-faced balloon that trailed behind her. The balloon had accordion legs and paper feet that made it "walk." With its cartoon grin, it seemed mocking and ridiculous. Lise tried to smile and chat cheerfully. It was as if she had rehearsed this scenario and had no idea how to veer away from her carefully prepared script. Later, I found out that she had been quite traumatized, never having witnessed such horror before in her young life.

In intensive care, Nicholas continued to suffer spasm and difficulty breathing, but it was not quite so bad with the stronger drugs on offer there. A little parent room down the hall was meant for use by neonatal intensive care mums and dads. But luckily, the room was empty and someone had abandoned a crumpled sheet on the sofa. I curled up inside the sheet and dozed off for a couple of hours. I staggered back into the blinding light of the treatment bays and to my baby boy, all wires and quiet beeping. He began to stir and I held his head, trying not to touch his swaddling bandages, by now with patches of brownish blood showing through. I sang "You are my sunshine, my only sunshine; you make me happy when skies are grey…" Suddenly a loud voice interrupted my intimate reverie with Nicholas. It was the curly-haired surgical resident. He moved towards us and barked, "What are you doing here!"

"I beg your pardon?" I asked dumbly.

"Who told you to leave the ward and come to ICU?"

I stared, fascinated, at a vein in his neck that was throbbing.

"The recommending consultant told us to come here. He arranged it."

"That doctor is NOT your doctor, I am! Your son is on the surgical team and I AM the surgeon in charge!" I might have laughed at this young underling's puffed-up ego, but instead I turned back to Nick and ignored him. The doctor swept out of the room in a swirl of indignation. I felt oddly disembodied and slightly amazed at this man's poor manners. I resumed my song, "You'll never know dear how much I love you, please don't take my sunshine away."

Official reports reflect so little of human drama. Here is what was written on Nicholas' discharge summary: "The patient was admitted to the hospital and the next day was taken for operation Nissen fundoplication and Stamm gastrostomy. He tolerated the procedure without complication. He was admitted to Pediatrics again and patient was having spasmodic attacks. The parents were very worried, so he was brought down to ICU for further management for his pain. A consultation with the gastroenterology physician regarding the problem was done and he suggested to continue the patient on Lorazepam and Demerol."

Days later, a specialist feeding nurse took me aside to show me how to use the feeding tube. There was a plastic bag with a length of tubing protruding from one end, plastic syringes and a radio-sized electric feeding pump. The nurse explained that I must wash my hands with Zest soap before beginning the preparation. She showed me how to prime the length of tubing without flooding the tiny drip chamber. Next came the demonstration of how to fit the chamber into a slot in the pump, lock it in place, and then program the pump with the desired drip speed, total dose and total volume. Finally, she showed me what to do if Nicholas felt sick. "He will retch, but won't be able to vomit except out of his tube. You can just let his stomach contents drain into a kitchen cup if he feels unwell," she said breezily. I was still wondering about the Zest soap, but I must have nodded my head to register an acceptable level of comprehension because after teaching me how to clean the tubing with dish soap, clear water and finally white vinegar, she exited the room, leaving me to pack up all the mysterious equipment. Just before leaving for home, a patient copy of the discharge note was thrust into my hand. The contact details for the nutrition specialist were pointed out to me in case of emergency. It was a number that I would come to know better than any other.

None of us knew then that when reflux is caused by intestinal incoordination below the stomach, preventing reflux by capping off the esophagus is like capping an active volcano. Nicholas began to retch as we turned into our driveway. Nick's feeding tube was inserted into his abdomen through a piercing in his tummy. A small, water-filled balloon that lodged against the lining of his stomach prevented the tube from popping out, much like the back of an earring stud. I would mix powdered formula with water, then decant it into a plastic bag attached to a long tube. I primed the tubing as I was instructed. The pump was similar to an IV pump and could be programmed to dispense the correct amount of feed over a period of hours by dripping slowly through a chamber in the mechanism. Nicholas continued to scream often throughout the night and one night, about eleven o'clock, I heard a quiet but unnatural coughing and choking sound from his room. I ran into Nicholas' bedroom and turned on the light. Nick was retching violently and struggling to breathe. Instinctively, I went to turn off the pump, but the feed bag was empty. Almost a litre of formula had disappeared. I struggled to comprehend how a feed meant to drip slowly over eight hours could be gone in under half an hour — I had only started the pump minutes before. As my eyes scanned the length of tubing, a terrible realization dawned on me. I had connected the feed, but forgotten to wind the tubing around the pump mechanism, so all the formula had raced through the tubing, unimpeded, by gravity. I pulled apart the coupling and the pressure in Nicholas' stomach caused his Foley catheter to snake wildly, spraying the ceiling with formula. "I'm sorry, Nicholas, I'm so sorry," I sobbed. I held him, rocking, as we both wept.

Aside from the effects of my exhaustion, Nicholas was suffering from a strange set of recurring symptoms, known to me, but inexplicable by all the science at our disposable. After a change of his Foley catheter, he would be all right for a couple of weeks. One day, he would retch maybe a couple of times and this behaviour signalled the start of a total intolerance of anything in his stomach, including water. I began to predict how many days it would be till even a teaspoon of water would cause bilious vomiting. In hospital, Nicholas would remain on IV fluids for three or four days, followed by the slow introduction of clear fluids and half-strength formula. Even though there was never anything functionally wrong with the catheter, often a change to a new one would cure his misery. All of these symptoms were a great mystery to me and to Nick's physicians.

Despite numerous hospital stays and a myriad of tests, Nicholas continued to be very ill and unable to digest his formula. In July 1992, his nutritionist wrote: "Nicholas has significant problems with gastrointestinal symptomatology including episodic retching, vomiting, pain and ongoing severe constipation. We have tried various motility medications and antacid medication with only limited success. His gastrostomy [feeding tube] appears to be utilized to provide between 30–50% of calories when he is relatively well and will provide more calories and fluid when he is having difficulty." Most of the time, Nicholas was having "difficulty."

Nicholas turned two years old on August 30, 1990. Four days later, early on September 3, rain pelted down as a yellow schoolbus pulled up in front of our house. I remember one thing: standing in my doorway, waving, looking at his little face through the foggy bus window. His head was tossed back, his mouth open in a scream I couldn't hear. I waved and blew kisses, thinking, "My God, what am I doing letting him go off like this?" And then, "How wonderful to have quiet, coffee, a newspaper!"

At 10 a.m. that same morning, the telephone rang. It was Moira, the school director at Cumberland Hub. "Now I don't want you to worry, but Nicholas is in an ambulance on his way to Children's Hospital. We think he has had a seizure. He fell asleep in his wheelchair and we couldn't wake him up. We called the fire department, you remember it's just across the street…they couldn't wake him up either. I told the ambulance driver that you would meet them at Emergency."

Driving while sobbing isn't easy, especially on a rainy day. But I managed to arrive at Emergency before Nicholas. I waited, imagining him on a stretcher, eyes rolled back with horribly jerking limbs.

I heard him before I saw him. The ambulance attendant held him out to me, explaining over his wails that he had woken up halfway to the hospital and screamed like a banshee ever since. Oh, here was my boy, he was all right. He was himself. I hadn't realized how frightened I had been that a seizure, something I knew nothing about, would somehow lobotomize him and render him unrecognizable. I thought that seizures inevitably caused more brain damage. I held him tightly, breathing deeply with relief at his wholeness.

Although the EEG test looked normal, the neurologist said, yes, it was probably a seizure. It might happen again today, in a month or never again. If you insist on medication, she said, it is Phenobarbital, but it slows learning development. I thanked her very much for the information and went home without a prescription. Years went by before I could hear a telephone ring without my heart pounding.

The next day, I brought Nicholas to school myself and stayed with him. My jaw was still set against this school and the diagnosis for Nick's learning that it represented. But I sat in this sunny, quiet room listening to Beethoven. Only two other children were in class: one in a hammock swinging gently and the other stacking blocks on his wheelchair tray, his teacher whispering encouragement. I had to admit that this was the perfect place for Nicholas to gently begin his schooling. I was determined that a mainstream classroom was his future, but for now, the Cumberland Hub would keep him safe and soothed.

After a year of quiet caring in that sunny, warm room with its woven hammock for gentle "sing and swing" therapy, I began to explore preschool options in my neighbourhood.

After the seizure, I had decided the bus was unsafe for Nick, and the Cumberland Hub was more than half an hour from home, which meant I was spending two hours a day driving. I was thrilled when Nicholas was accepted as an exceptional student at a local church preschool. But I hadn't realized that in transferring Nick to his new preschool, he would lose all his therapies. If physio, speech or occupational therapies were going to be part of his weekly routine, I would have to book these appointments at the hospital treatment centre. Mainstream school and therapies didn't mix, I was told. The trade-off to have Nick in the mainstream translated into a terribly punishing schedule for us both.

Fighting to streamline services at one location was my first political battle and my first victory. Eventually, Nicholas would stay at school after hours two days a week for occupational and physiotherapies. Therapists would train the school staff how to engage Nicholas with his classroom and its contents. They came with ideas and equipment that made it possible for Nick to paint, play with blocks and use the outdoor playground. Nicholas was happiest watching the boisterous activity of his classmates. His report identified a principal strength as "smiles a lot." I was annoyed at how patronizing this sounded with its inference that passivity and simple-mindedness constituted academic achievement.

But fatigue and a nagging sensation of mild nausea distracted me from my usual ire. I was pregnant. Jim and I had been trying for another child, and the previous year I had experienced the sadness of a "missed abortion" — our embryo had died in utero. But this baby was meant to be and nine months later, our Natalie was born, a sister for Nicholas. A few moments after her appearance in the operating room, the doctors placed Natalie on the steel table to wash her. Lying on her stomach, she pushed up with her arms, lifting her upper body off the table. Natalie was only a few minutes old and already she could perform a move that Nicholas could only imagine! Mothering a healthy baby was a revelation to me. With each of Natalie's milestones, the extent of Nicholas' differences was revealed in harsh light. With her first steps, I cheered and cried tears of amazement and pride mingled with sadness for Nick's loss.

But babies have a way of seducing those who care for them and Natalie firmly established her personhood almost immediately. I was more nervous than a first-time mother, thinking I was incapable of sensing what a "normal" baby might need or want. Soon I knew her hungry cry from her painful ones. I knew her frustration with confinement — suddenly the world had shifted to make room for another kind of future for our family.

CHAPTER TWO

Amartya Sen and the Capability Approach

In many ways, the peripatetic lifestyle of diplomacy has been good for our family. As a young couple, our first posting was to Moscow in 1978. Living with limited freedoms there taught us the value of resilience and creativity when faced with oppression. Later, a second posting in Washington, DC, was memorable for career-building and weekends at the East Coast seaside with friends. But when Nicholas and Natalie arrived in our family, the idea of packing up seemed daunting, yet I was determined to try. London beckoned and four years in England proved to us that not only could we travel, but we could also thrive in a foreign land. We returned to Ottawa and lived quietly for ten years. Then in 2006, Jim told me that the prime minister had asked him to be high commissioner in London, and I was thrilled. I play-acted thinking about the offer, and then shouted "Yes!" as we laughed and hugged each other and the children. On August 27, 2006, we arrived in London and moved in to No. 3 Grosvenor Square, the official residence of the Canadian high commissioner.

Until recently, I had not considered writing a book about our family life with Nicholas. I always believed that Nick's disability was an accident of nature and had no bearing on society in general. I knew from experience that when I began to talk to most people about my daily life, their eyes would glaze over and they would turn away, muttering excuses. Anyway, the disability community did not need another piece of misery porn or worse still, inspirational lit. But all that changed in 2008 during a casual conversation with Dr. Susan Hodgett of Ulster University in Belfast. Susan had nominated my husband, Jim, to receive an honorary doctorate from her university on account of his own and Canada's role in forging an enduring peace in Northern Ireland (Jim had worked on the peace process during our previous posting to the UK in the 1990s).

As Susan and I stood waiting for Jim to be capped and gowned, we chatted about my interest in learning lessons for disability and nonprofit work from those working in the area of development and extreme poverty. Susan breathed in and said quietly, "You should know about Amartya Sen." As she began to describe Sen's ideas, I almost felt the earth shift underfoot. I realized that using Sen's ideas of human freedom and potential gave Nicholas' life and my own experience an important ethical connection to the rest of society. If his ideas could be harnessed as a language to speak about having the freedom to live a life of value *even for us*, then this had to be important to anyone who cared about fairness and justice in society generally. Suddenly, I saw that we were not just the victims of bad luck — rather we had something fundamental in common with the oppressed groups in Sen's research. Surely this was something worth exploring and writing about.

Amartya Sen won the Nobel Prize in 1998 for his work in combining the disciplines of economics and philosophy. He advocated dispensing with the usual measures of assessing poverty, such as household income and GDP, believing they offered insufficient insight into the real causes of human misery and injustice. He began to explore poverty through the lens of the choices or freedoms that individuals have within circumstances of deprivation. The key idea of the Capability Approach is that social arrangements should expand people's capabilities, or their freedom to promote whatever activities and lifestyle they value. Sen argues that the central concern of having a decent and valued life worth living is that of freedom. It is not money and it is not "accomplishments." The approach examines the range of possibilities for human flourishing within a given set of circumstances, especially circumstances involving adversity.

An example that Sen often uses to illustrate his Capability Approach is that of two starving people. One is in the last stages of a hunger strike, the other a victim of a prolonged drought. Measured without benefit of Sen's approach, these two individuals appear identical. It is Sen's approach that offers us insight into their very different options or possible choices for action to alleviate their suffering. Sen calls this their "capability space." In his Nobel Prize–winning autobiography, Sen wrote: "The approach explored sees individual advantage not merely as opulence or utility, but primarily in terms of the lives people manage to live and the freedom they have to choose the kind of life they have reason to value. The basic idea here is to pay attention to the actual 'capabilities' that people end up having. These capabilities depend both on our physical and mental characteristics as well as on social opportunities and influences (and can thus serve as the basis not only of assessment of personal advantage, but also of efficiency and equity of social policies)."[1]

Significantly, Sen uses the word *equity* rather than *equality* — an important distinction for those concerned with disability. The word *equality* applied to people with handicapping conditions has often led to abandonment, such as the child in a mainstream school with no support services because extra help would be *unequal* treatment. It seems to me that equity is a much more helpful aspiration — one that encompasses the recognition of capacity and resilience on the part of vulnerable individuals, as well as those who love and support them. This approach shifts attention away from the medical model of disability to a view of personal freedom and the choices that one has, given the effects of impairment on those available choices. Effectively, the disability experience is positioned alongside gender and age as just one aspect of human diversity.

For me, Sen's Capability Approach represents a lens through which I can assess the value of my life, and understand my choices in relation to programs, services and policies that have affected us throughout my son's life. Sen speaks of the "freedom to live the life you value and have reason to value." I had a life mapped out for myself before Nicholas was born, a life that I imagined I valued. The circumstances of our family life with Nicholas forced me to reconsider my values and my reasons for holding those values. In his body of work, Sen is responding to the horror of extreme poverty and famine. I have never been hungry. I live in a beautiful home and in many regards have led a highly privileged adult life. Yet the questions that Sen's Capability Approach poses about human potential and the barriers to achieving it are the cornerstone of understanding the experience of our family. If Sen's idea of the capability to live a life worth living is dependent on one's physical and mental characteristics as well as one's social opportunities and influences, how could a family like ours possibly survive, much less thrive? My son's physical characteristics cause him to be completely dependent on others.

Although Amartya Sen has focused on issues relating to poverty and justice, he has also spoken about disability. At a World Bank Conference on Disability in 2004, he lamented the failure of theories of justice to address the issue of disability adequately. In his keynote speech at that conference, Sen explored the relationship of wealth, disability, freedom and justice:

> Wealth or income is not something we value for its own sake. A person with severe disability need not really be judged to be more advantaged than an able-bodied person, even if he or

she has a higher level of income or wealth than the thoroughly
fit person. We have to examine the overall capability that any
person has to lead the kind of life she has reason to want to
lead, and this requires that attention be paid to her personal
characteristics (and this includes her disabilities, if any) as
well as to her income and other resources, since both can
influence her actual capabilities. To ground a theory of justice
on the informational foundation of opulence and income distribution would be a confusion of ends and means: income and
opulence are things that we seek "for the sake of something
else," as Aristotle put it.[2]

Here, Sen is distinguishing between "earning handicaps" and "conversion handicaps," or how one is able to
convert money into good living. Giving someone with
disabilities a million dollars doesn't give them a good life
if the money stays in the bank and the individual sits at
home unable to convert his riches into enjoyable living.
It is easy to see why, for people with disabilities, this line
of thinking is extremely helpful in understanding the
injustices that plague them. But Sen does not limit his
definition of a conversion handicap to finances. He also
points out that social facilities are a "common good,"
which are often not accessible to people with disabling
conditions. Community centres, schools and churches
may exist, but if someone like Nicholas cannot get into
these buildings, they will hardly contribute to his wellbeing. For people who require care, it is their loved ones
who naturally take it upon themselves to mediate a deal
for turning community resources into good living.

My own experience tells me that converting money into fulfillment requires imagination and self-discipline. Money squandered, like any gift, can lead to misery (as in the case of gambling addicts). But the same could be said of disability. That particular fact of life can be converted into a positive force that reveals the best in human qualities, such as determination, resilience, creativity and compassion. It is a serious misconception to believe that money automatically translates to good living, or that disability converts to misery. Mark Oakley, our priest and old friend, put it best: "It is not circumstances that make or destroy a life. Anyone who has survived the death of a lover, the loss of a position, the end of a dream, the enmity of a friend knows that. …It is the way we live each of the circumstances of life, the humdrum as well as the extraordinary, the daily as well as the defining moments, that defines the quality of our lives. Each of us has the latitude to live life either well or poorly. Ironically enough, it is a matter of decision. And that decision is ours."

The American philosopher Eva Feder Kittay has spent most of her professional life writing about what it means to mother her daughter, Sesha. Sesha is now a grown woman and because of a severe developmental disability and cerebral palsy is completely reliant on others. Kittay weighs in on Sen's ideas and how they might affect families such as mine. In thinking about equality, she identifies the fact that all people are not alike with the same abilities as a starting point. In her discussion of Sen's ideas, she explains: "What we want to insure, claims Sen, is not merely that everyone has access to the same goods with fair equality of opportunity, but that we equalize each person's capability to function freely."[3] This is true equity wherein individuals are free to convert *all* the aspects of their lives into good (or bad) living. If Sen's ideas of freedom, capability and justice had been taken as both a means and an end to disability policy, programs and services, how would Nicholas' early years have been different?

More than two years after my first conversation with Susan Hodgett at the University of Ulster, I managed to make contact with Amartya Sen of Trinity College, Cambridge. With the assistance of generous, well-placed friends and a fair amount of tenacity on my part, I had managed to organize the hottest date of my life. I needed to ask Professor Sen if my application of his Capability Approach for disability in a developed world setting was valid. I wondered whether proposing the idea of a maximum capability set (especially in the area of education) was appropriate. After all, this approach was originally conceived in order to understand minimum levels of capability in the case of people living in circumstances of extreme poverty.

On January 21, 2010, I found myself boarding the train from London to Cambridge. The train was nearly empty, so I spread my papers out on the table opposite my seat. I looked at them and wondered if my meeting with this Nobel Prizewinner would result in my manuscript being left in a Trinity College wastebasket. I arrived early and found what I thought was the correct waiting room. I attempted to compose myself by pretending to read my notes. I moved to the bottom of the stairway that seemed to lead into an upstairs dining room. Suddenly from a lower hall, Professor Sen appeared. We climbed the stairs as he explained the dining arrangements and the menu. Being unfamiliar with academia, let alone casual conversations with Nobel Prizewinners, I wondered if we would have a chance to discuss my book at all. Other academics sat at the long tables and we took our places amongst them. As Professor Sen chatted amicably to others at the table, I smiled nervously and listened. Finally, we finished our dessert and Sen suggested that we retire to the reading room to discuss my project. We found two armchairs by the fire and breathlessly, I asked my questions — was the Capability Approach a valid lens for my family experience? Yes. "It would be a shame if the approach had nothing to offer anyone living above a subsistence level," he said. Could I apply the approach in an effort to include maximum levels of opportunity and choice? Yes, definitely. I asked his advice on how to present complex ideas in a coherent way for general audiences without losing authenticity. "Ah," he replied. "Generally I find that readers are generous. If you express a fact or opinion, they will assume you've done the work. Don't worry so much." I left Trinity that day feeling relieved and resolved. After my conversation with Professor Sen, I was sure that the capability framework would present disability as just one aspect of human complexity in a world where we all interact differently with our physical, economic, social and cultural environments. This was a belief that I considered to be true and a value that I will always hold precious.

CHAPTER THREE

Beginning to Think Differently

I remember being a parent representative on a committee to restructure local services for families like mine. Nicholas was in nursery school at the time. All the heads of social and health-care facilities were at the table and I suggested that we offer direct payments to parents so that they could choose which services they wanted. The director of the children's rehabilitation centre looked at me, alarmed, and asked, "But what if they buy leather pants with the money?" I wondered aloud whether employers would voice the same worry about their workers' paycheques.

John Maynard Keynes once remarked, "Practical men, who believe themselves to be quite exempt from any intellectual influences, are usually the slaves of some defunct economist."[4] I would suggest that those who believe social change can be debated without consideration for its most vulnerable members are slaves to defunct philosophers.

Traditionally, economists have measured standard of living by the ability to buy a basket of commodities or by utility, understood as happiness. The Capability Approach focuses on the kind of life that people manage to lead and whether that life has value to the individual, from their perspective, not ours. This way of looking at the rich and poor of the world takes into account how some poor people can be happy and how those with monetary wealth may be miserable.

Sen's approach is particularly helpful in assessing the wellbeing of people with disabilities and their families, because their values, aspirations and circumstances are so different from the status quo. They may not be able to convert wealth into good living if there is no access to the outside world and its riches.

On the other hand, they may have very little of what is considered important by others, yet they are happy and healthy. Furthermore, people with disabilities are little known to the general public and as such, are likely to be misunderstood. When the Ontario government gave us a little money for respite care, often I didn't hire helpers, I hired a cleaning lady — especially when Nicholas was ill or in pain. I wanted to be with him and he wanted his mum. Sen is concerned more with a person's interests than his or her actions or behaviours.

Now that Nicholas is an adult, the extent to which he pursues interests and enjoys a life that he values is wholly dependent on the assistance of caregivers, together with technological support. Nicholas is reliant on technology to eat, breathe, speak and remain pain free. He is tube-fed by an electric pump and uses an oxygen-saturation monitor at night to alert the carer if he stops breathing. Nicholas has used a switch-operated speaking computer and has used adapted software to learn at school. Recently, by directing his helper on the computer, Nicholas completed an online IT course and he used that knowledge to become a seller on eBay. Nick's exploration of the Internet, with the help of his carers, has even allowed him to discover the experience of being able-bodied in virtual worlds.

Trying to imagine Nicholas' life without technology is difficult, but not impossible. Back in 1998 when Nicholas was ten, much of eastern Canada was declared to be in a state of emergency. Over the course of eleven days, almost 40 millimetres of freezing rain fell, crushing power lines and toppling the entire power grid serving Ottawa and Montreal. While the temperature dropped and we huddled beside our fireplace, the realization dawned on me that without electricity, I could not feed Nicholas. Nick is tube-fed and his pump is electric. His principal mode of communication at that time was a speaking computer, operated via head switches. Without power, Nicholas could not speak. Without heat in the house, he began to shiver. A natural disaster suddenly caused Nick to become much, much more disabled than I had ever known him to be. Luckily, a hotel unaffected by the power outage made room for Jim, me and both children as well as Goldie, our dog. We were all delighted to have an all-inclusive "adventure holiday." Nicholas has a life that he values, and that value is almost wholly derived from assistive devices, including computer technology. Without electrical power, Nicholas cannot eat or speak. Even worse for him, he is completely cut off from the rest of the world. The ice storm was a lesson in dependency for everyone, especially the frail. Thank goodness for us, it lasted less than a week.

Left to his own devices, Nicholas would die of thirst and starvation. Left to the government, he would exist, but not flourish. With government support and the care of family and friends, Nick has a future as an active citizen whose contributions are valued by all those around him. The Capability Approach in the context of extreme poverty is very much about minimum levels of freedom or *operating space* within which a person can function and aspire to achieve goals. But Sen has deliberately been vague about how his approach might be implemented and assessed in the real world. I've decided to apply the principles in their broadest sense and in the comparative context of my own culture and neighbourhood. Sen advocates using his approach to expand capabilities by removing injustices. But his theories do not directly address the case of disability where physical and mental capacities vary so widely. So, in the context of my own family experience, I have decided to use the Capability Approach to expand the capability space of my family to its maximum, rather than to a minimum. I do so because that is the level I have come to expect as rightfully mine in Canada and the UK as an educated, middle-class person. So, for my family, "What is a good life?" followed by "How can we get one?" are good places to start.

CHAPTER FOUR

A Plan for the Future

For me, the dawn of the millennium held more fears than just that of a possible Y2K disaster. Nicholas was almost twelve years old and had survived multiple near-death experiences. Clearly, my son was a survivor. So, the mantra of my worry, "What if he dies?" was slowly becoming "What if he lives?"

In 1999, I began to help my old friend Kathleen Jordan in her efforts to plan a safe and happy future for her son, Christopher. Chris Jordan is Nicholas' senior by almost fifteen years, and through him I had a glimpse of our family's future. I didn't like what I saw. Kathleen and her husband, Bill, still looked after Chris at home. They managed to cope with almost daily emergencies, even as they endured failing health themselves. By that time Kathleen had begun to organize parents in Ottawa, telling us about a revolutionary idea from Vancouver called PLAN. Together, we became convinced that this organization could save our lives and teach society how to be more caring in the bargain.

PLAN: AN IDEA IS BORN

In the late 1980s, a small group of people began meeting together in Vancouver, British Columbia, to think about futures that were not their own. Each of them had a son or daughter with a developmental disability, and together, they considered these sons and daughters. They considered their joys and their fears. They considered their dreams and their safety. They considered their places in the world. All of the parents bore well-earned scars from the political battles and guerilla actions they had fought to enable their children to receive the support they needed: schooling; housing, medical and psychological care; money. They knew the system well, could negotiate its highways and its alleys and its cul-de-sacs. But they were tired. And they were afraid, because they realized that advances in health care meant they would have to face a problem few people in history had ever faced. Their disabled children were likely to outlive them. Despite their hard-won expertise, their intricate knowledge of the agencies and organizations meant to serve the disabled community, they knew that, sooner or later, their children would be without their advocacy, cast adrift in an institutional world that could not protect them from the devastating personal and systemic loneliness that the parents feared the most.

In many ways the small group of parents had itself been born of loneliness. The group was the work of a peculiar synchronicity. Each member had suffered recent and profound loss: death, illness, divorce — disorienting chords that had left them bruised and battered individually, but also open to thinking about the world and working with each other in a new way.

And a new way of thinking and working was exactly what they sought. They sensed that the current model of providing for the disabled, the familiar twentieth-century concoction of institutional service and legal contest, provided few answers to their sons' and daughters' most meaningful questions and yearnings. And they knew that the nonprofits that worked within the disabled community were deeply embedded in this model, both mentally ("How else could we do this work?") and financially, since they received most of their money from government agencies. In fact, group members had been intimately involved in many of these nonprofits, founding them, working for them, sitting on their boards. They knew a lot about governance and policy and legal and financial issues. They had a particular expertise in estate planning; several people in the group were involved in workshops that helped parents develop wills and trusts appropriate for supporting disabled offspring. But they all felt that the structures they had participated in and helped create were missing something vital.

Jack Collins was there. He says, "We all spent years building these nonprofit organizations that were supposed to be providing services to our children, but they did not really look at the needs of the person . . . [Our local association] didn't offer anything but programs which suited the needs of the association." He talks about his daughter Pam: "Whenever we asked for something, they put her in a training program." He pauses and stares at his hands. "They trained her to bake muffins once."

Jack says that what the members of this small group

shared, in addition to a particular family experience with disability, was "complete dissatisfaction with this system." They wanted to create something entirely different, an organization, a movement, a way of understanding the world that would secure the futures of their children and others like them by acknowledging and responding to their deepest human needs, not simply their superficial predicaments.

The group, however, had little notion of what that something might be. So they talked with each other and they visited different programs. They opened, without mercy, their own assumptions and wounds. Funded by research and planning grants, they spent three years in deep inquiry, immersed in profoundly honest, occasionally contentious, dialogue with each other and with the world around them. Slowly, a fresh way of understanding the disabled community and the organizations meant to serve that community began to emerge. A fledgling model of a different kind of organization with a different way of seeing the world took shape. Like all fledglings, the model was damp and awkward and fuzzy in places. But in 1989, with a tiny office, and still only the vaguest idea of what it would all mean eventually, the Planned Lifetime Advocacy Network, PLAN, was born.[5]

Like all innovative, simple and brilliant ideas, this model of support began with an unexpected question. Rather than asking who would look after their sons and daughters, or who would pay for their care, these parents asked, "What IS a good life?" Their consensus was that a good life for people with disabilities is not very different from a good life for anyone else: friends and family, a place of one's own, financial security, choice and the ability to make a contribution to society are the key ingredients.

First and foremost in realizing these values or freedoms in the lives of people with disabilities is an understanding that caring relationships are the key to a good life. Furthermore, these wise parents recognized that people with disabilities often find it difficult to forge and sustain friendships. But caring relationships alone are not enough to sustain a good life — individual contributions must be enabled and valued in families and communities.

Finally, PLAN's model to support children with disabilities as they age is directed and financed by families. The portion that is not paid by families is raised through charitable fundraising, coupled with awareness training for the public about our children's civic contributions. Operational funds remain safe from cutbacks by steering clear of government funding — the family has total control of the entire process. The PLAN model is unique in the sense that it encompasses the aspirations of the whole family, not just the person with a disability.

I rely heavily on my friends to enrich my life, through good times and bad. My friends leave care packages at my door when I am ill, they pray for my elderly mother if she is hospitalized and they laugh with me over dinner. I want Nicholas to have that same kind of support after Jim and I are gone. I know that other friends or family members can never replace Jim and me in Nicholas' life, and I also know that Natalie cannot shoulder that responsibility alone. The letters in PLAN stand for Planned Lifetime Advocacy Networks. What do network members do?

In the early years of PLAN, the status quo for people requiring care in their community was to receive services and participate in programs funded by tax dollars. No one imagined that people with disabilities had anything to give back to society. But anyone who loves a vulnerable individual will be happy to list that person's gifts and contributions to family and the wider community. For anyone who has the capacity to act at all, a valued contribution gives meaning and confers value to that person's life. Contribution equals citizenship became a core value of the PLAN movement. At the Ottawa PLAN parent group (Lifetime Networks Ottawa), I organized a fundraising tour of beautiful private gardens in the city. Any activity that I undertook had to showcase our values. So each garden on the tour had a greeter (one of our children) who took tickets and welcomed the public. Nicholas performed this function at our own neighbourhood garden. Even though he had required some assistance, I noticed that everyone was careful to thank Nick for his helpful participation.

Over the past twenty years, PLAN network members have been acting in the best interests of a friend with a disability by:

- Monitoring the formal programs and services that our relatives receive
- Becoming effective advocates

- Serving as executors and trustees or as advisors
- Offering help and support in making important decisions
- Responding promptly and effectively to crisis
- Solving problems and handling the unexpected
- Carrying out the wishes of parents

All of these roles are shared and performed by a group of individuals who truly care for the person at the centre of the network. Network members are not paid, nor are they volunteers. They are friends. And PLAN exists to ensure that network members function together as *good* friends of the person at the heart of the network over his or her entire lifetime.

PLAN offers families the tools for creating a future that includes enduring friendships as well as a financial plan to support a good life for their relative. Families pay for these services and leave money in their will to ensure the enduring integrity of their personal vision.

The values of the PLAN movement continue to inspire me; the founding families unwittingly went about identifying and creating the circumstances of human freedom for their children with disabilities. The PLAN model is very much a Capability Approach model — it is least restrictive, but most supportive. But at the moment, despite the efforts of those involved with advocating for measures to encourage active and caring citizenship, the issues relating to a good life for people with disabilities are of little interest to those unaffected by disabling conditions.

People may read in the papers about another tragic

case of a parent who, being overwhelmed, takes the life of a son or daughter with disabilities. But they won't read this story and relate it to the care of their own aging parent. The fact is, in the years ahead, all people with a need for care in the community will be in competition for ever-scarcer resources from the public purse. And in a climate of limited resources for care, everyone needs friends.

CHAPTER FIVE

Eldercare

Like other baby boomers, I worry about my elderly mother. I am fifty-five years old and my mother is eighty-eight. I live in England and my mother resides in a Montreal seniors' residence. Luckily, my sister lives in Montreal. But last year, when my mother became seriously ill, I flew home to help. Long-distance caring is turning into the norm for contemporary families.

My mother has savings that allow her to live in her own apartment, with help available, if she needs it. Some of her costs are covered by Canada Pension benefits combined with a small work pension, and those benefits combined with her personal savings cover her living costs. There is no doubt that her circumstances are more than adequate to meet her needs and aspirations. What will be the future of my generation?

In the next twenty-five years, the population of Canada will double. According to Statistics Canada, 18.4 percent of all Canadians have "moderate to poor" functional health, likely necessitating some form of assistance for daily living.[6] Fully three-quarters of a million Canadians (22 percent of seniors) require intensive care due to a chronic health problem or a physical disability. And increasingly, to be old in Canada means to live out one's final years in poverty. The combination of a rapidly aging demographic and the reluctance of governments at all levels to launch new social programs spells continuing suffering and neglect for the most vulnerable seniors of today, and even greater hardship down the road for many Canadians now in early middle age.[7]

The novelist Martin Amis made the news in the British papers when he picked a fight with the grey power of the UK's aging population, calling for euthanasia "booths" on street corners where the elderly can terminate their lives with "a martini and a medal." Never shy of controversy, the author asserted that in Britain, there is a civil war coming between the young and the old. "They'll be a population of demented very old people, like an invasion of terrible immigrants, stinking out the restaurants and cafés and shops," he said. Amis admitted that his remarks were "satirical," but otherwise defended his pro-euthanasia stance.[8]

There is no doubt that care is headed for the dubious distinction of being a rare commodity. Like energy, clean air and water, there won't be enough to go around.

But I disagree with the premise of Martin Amis' argument. I don't believe that this looming crisis will *pit* young against old or the elderly against the disabled. We love our relatives who require care. No loving son or daughter could conceive of promoting the early demise of their parent.

And Amis has failed to grasp one more crucial point — there is money to be made in the new growth industry of care provision. There is gold in all that silver.

Jim Maxmin and Dr. Allan "Chip" Teel developed a practical and innovative solution to ensuring the safety and security of senior citizens in rural Maine. In a state with very few resources to fund social care, Maxmin and Teel decided to look for inspiration in unexpected places. Their models for change were iTunes, Craigslist, Facebook, Wikipedia…and Obama's campaign. These transformational and democratizing platforms offered the free sharing of resources, knowledge and support. Elder Power is Maxmin and Teel's big idea for our aging population. It is a network of elders supporting elders, connected to a system of community volunteers, technology, semiprofessionals, and doctors. For seniors with dementia, sensors and video cameras offer as much or as little monitoring as one chooses. Computer access enables social networking as well as links to doctors and a community call centre.

> It's the elders themselves, along with other network volunteers, who provide social support: a phone call to remind you to turn on the football game, an all-day visit, a plumber, home diagnostics. Rides are provided to lunch gatherings each day — with students at the local elementary and high school, in a restaurant, a church, on a picnic — and to classes and clinics held at the local residential care facility. Soon there will be a fully dedicated video channel called ElderPower TV where Chip and others can broadcast advice. There are plans for mobile

medical care — paid for in part by subscriptions from other community members who want those house calls, too — with profits returned to the network.[9]

Maxmin and Teel are not the only innovators working on the problem of caring for our aging population. Vickie Cammack of the PLAN Institute has developed a new online tool called Tyze to help family and friends ensure the wellbeing of their vulnerable relative. Thirty years of building real time networks for families across the country gave Vickie the knowledge and experience of what makes good support networks tick. Tyze networks are networks with a purpose. They can be completely customized to anyone's personal circumstances and needs.

In the trial stages of Tyze, one of the first sites was created for an elderly gentleman who needed support, but lived far away from his family. Charles was eighty-seven when his health took a turn. His children called often, but felt keenly the miles between their far-flung homes and the quiet Scottish town where their dad lived alone. It was his son John who suggested Tyze. At first, his sisters didn't like the idea. They didn't use email much and were uncomfortable with how sites like Facebook made peoples' lives so public. But John assured them that Tyze was private and simple to use.

In less than a week, Tyze had proved its usefulness. Sitting on the other side of the world, it was a powerful thing to read a note from the osteopath who had treated Charles that morning. The woman who cleaned Charles' house also posted. The daily stories that came through Tyze from Scotland drew a picture for the family of Charles' diminishing coping skills. Within days, the sisters were converted. "It's almost as good as being there with Dad when we get your posts," one of them wrote.

The site became a global bulletin board where contact numbers were posted along with a calendar of appointments and visits. John and his sisters especially liked the way the site forged connections between them and the professionals paid to treat their dad. The osteopath became an important ally while John and his sisters navigated an unfamiliar health-care system in a foreign country. And for the professionals working with Charles, connection with the family brought them closer to this retired banker and much-loved father.

Everyone needs care at some point in their life. The roots of Tyze are in the disability community, but its helpful benefits are already being felt around the globe with seniors, single mothers and anyone else who needs extra help to be safe, healthy and happy. We use Tyze with Nicholas to coordinate the myriad of care staff who work in our home 24/7. Every participant on the program has been invited by the administrator (in our case, that's me). Because the system was designed to accommodate highly personal information, it is completely secure. Tyze has a story facility that we use to update information about the online college course that Nicholas is currently doing. Medical appointments and transportation arrangements can be found in the calendar page, but so can special social events or hockey games. When a new medication is started, an alert goes out to all staff and if side effects are a worry, the prescribing physician is added to the network list until the situation stabilizes. The melding of formal supports (doctors, therapists, social workers, etc.) with informal supports (such as grandmothers, aunts, cousins) is the critical element in what makes Tyze helpful for us.

Long-term care in the community, if it is to be good care, must have excellent lines of communication between all parties. But somehow, up until now, communication has been stymied on account of misplaced notions of what defines a professional — in a home setting, the medical model of doctor/patient relations actually hinders good care. Anyone who has tried to navigate effective communications with doctors on behalf of an aging parent with diminishing capacities will know this. Loving family members have had their credibility questioned by virtue of being "emotionally involved." This archaic view that concerns of daily living are somehow separate from professional concerns is dealt a fatal blow by Tyze. With legions of families fulfilling the complex care needs of their relatives in their homes, a two-way, open, honest and mutually respectful dialogue must be enabled between people with long-term care needs, their families and the professionals who seek to support them. Caring for our parents has the potential to be the catalyst for transforming our society into a more caring and profitable society.

CHAPTER SIX

I Am Loved,
Therefore I Am

Whenever our family moves to a new country, or when Nicholas' age provokes a change in the government departments that serve his needs, we encounter the same frustrating wrangling. Social services representatives sit across the table from their counterparts from the Ministry of Health. When asked who will pay for Nick's care in the community, each points to the other and says, "It's *you*!" It never fails to shock me that Nicholas is *persona non grata*, at least as far as governments are concerned.

Where do dependent and vulnerable people belong in our society and why should anyone care about, much less pay for, their good life? If people with disabilities and their families are a case study in dependency issues and capability for our society, what factors constitute the measures for wellbeing?

Many parents will identify with me when I talk about Nicholas' contribution to the quality of my life, especially to my spiritual wellbeing. I am a better person for loving him and caring for him. But certainly I cannot say that because I have cared for my son, and consequently increased capacities for selflessness in myself by virtue of attending to his needs, that either of us would wish to claim *that* as his contribution to life in general. The idea of identifying care needs as a contribution because it makes the carer a better person is dealt with by the theologian and father of a child with severe disabilities, David A. Pailin: "Those who are looking for a reason to justify caring have not understood that love is a self-justifying and all-sufficient ground for certain types of behaviour. Those who remain puzzled by love (and even cynical about references to it) should therefore consider whether the contributory worth notion of value has blinded them to what is good in itself."[10] Pailin maintains that worth is received, not rooted in what a person can do or give. Pailin aligns the worth of people with severe disabilities with that of our worth in God's eyes. And, he points out, God doesn't assign worth on the basis of ability. The recognition and embodiment of unconditional love is enough.[11]

The hierarchy of the disability rights movement (paraplegics at the top and mental health and severe learning disabilities at the bottom) reflects society's comfort with the goodness of purposive and participatory action. A person with no ability to participate in this realm simply embodies need. But if a person has no capacity for purposive action, then it follows that they must be exempt from judgement. It is enough for that person simply to receive love.

Some activists in the disability movement defend the worth of those with cognitive disabilities by pointing to the "contribution of being." But that stance is rooted in what positive effects might be experienced by an able-bodied person while spending time with someone who seems unresponsive. "I love spending time with my aunt who has advanced Alzheimer's disease because we just sit together. I have a busy job and she helps to slow me down" is one story I heard to back up this theory.

But, what if this aunt had no visitors who enjoyed sitting with her? Does this woman's worth diminish the longer she lives without her capacity for reason? What if all her relatives were killed in an accident and there was no one left who remembered this elderly woman before the onset of her disease? In the case of the severest forms of disability, it may be too difficult to *imagine* an individual ever having capacity. How do we rate the worth of such souls? The theological anthropologist Hans Reinders expands on the idea of received love as the scorecard for worthiness. "The gift that profoundly disabled human beings have received is the gift of being, which is derived from the freedom of judgement. No entrance tickets are needed, no exams have to be passed. ...The gift of being is not an abstraction; it is the gift of being what you are."[12]

As well, American philosopher Eva Feder Kittay, who commented on Sen's work earlier in this book, is the mother of Sesha, a young woman with severe cognitive disabilities, and she is leading the charge amongst her colleagues for a consensus of human worth that includes her daughter. Dr. Kittay needs to be strong for a long and tough fight.

However, in his book *The Ethics of Killing: Problems*

at the Margins of Life, bio-ethicist Jeff McMahan refers to people with severe cognitive disabilities as having the moral value of a chimp.[13] In other places, he maintains that they have psychological capacities equivalent to those of a dog. Dr. McMahan is a professor of philosophy and ethics at Princeton University. His colleague at the Princeton University Center for Human Values, Dr. Peter Singer, offers samples of highly intelligent animal life to prove that severely cognitively impaired humans have less moral worth than some pigs. Drs. McMahan and Singer are well-known animal rights activists who want to throw light on the inconsistency of ethics that would sanction the slaughter of animals for food, yet protect and prolong the lives of people with inferior intellectual capacity to some nonhumans.

Consider this exchange with Eva Kittay, Peter Singer and Jeff McMahan at a 2008 Conference at Stony Brook University:

Peter Singer (directed at Eva Kittay) : You've said a couple of times and you said it again in response to the last question that you think that Jeff [McMahan] doesn't have the empirical stuff right, and you also said that in response to my comparison between humans and nonhuman animals. You put up Jeff's comments [in which McMahan puts forward a list of comparisons between "radically cognitively impaired" humans and nonhuman animals and then says] and so on and so forth. ...Then you said that "we can't wave our hands and then say and so on, because there is so much more to what it is to be human." You've said that a couple of times. So I am just wanting to ask you: Well, can you tell us some of these morally significant psychological capacities in which you think that human beings, and let's talk about real ones, so the ones who are "profoundly mentally retarded," to use that term, in which they are superior to...you sort of said, maybe chimpanzees and great apes are different...so let's say in which they are superior to pigs or dogs or animals of that sort. (Eva Kittay responds by shaking her head.) It's a factual question. You can't just shake your head. You have to put up or stop saying that.

Eva Kittay: [Y]ou asked me how is Sesha different from a — what did you say — a pig? And [when I first shook my head] you said, well, it's a factual question, "put up or shut up." The first thing I have to do when you ask me that question, is I have to get over.... a feeling of nausea. It's not that I'm not able to answer it intellectually, it's that I can't even get to the point emotionally, where I can answer that question. *(Pause)* Most of the time. When I say you can't just wave your hand and say "and so on," it's because there is so *much* to being human. There's the touch, there's the feel, there's the hug, there's the smile...there are so many ways of interacting. I don't think you need philosophy for this. You need *a very good writer*. ...This is why I just reject...[the]...idea that you [should] base moral standing on a list of cognitive capacities, or any kind of capacities. Because what it is to be human is not a bundle of capacities. It's a way that you *are*, a way you are in the world, a way you are with another. And I could adore my pig; I could dote on my pig. It would be something entirely different. And if you can't get that; if you can't understand that, then I'm not sure exactly what it is that you want to hear from that I could tell you. ...I'll keep trying because I think this is very important.

Jeff McMahan: Let me say something on behalf of Peter's [Singer's] point of view here. Peter has not said anything to deny the significance of a mother's relations to her own child. Nothing as far as I can tell. The question here is a question about what moral demands there are on other people. And the fact that you, Eva, have a relation with your daughter doesn't necessarily give other people the same set of reasons that you have to respond to your daughter in certain ways and to treat your daughter in certain ways. The question is: what is it about people like your daughter that makes moral demands on other people that nonhuman animals can make on any of us. That is the question that Peter is asking. He's not denying that you have a special relation to your daughter and that that is very significant for you in your life, significant for her, and so on, and that that's true of many other people. ...You know, Peter and I didn't come here to hurt anybody's feelings. We're here to try to understand things better. I'm trying very hard not to say anything offensive, something hurtful. I'm profoundly averse to making people miserable.

Eva Kittay: I know you're not trying to hurt anyone's feelings. I know Peter isn't trying to hurt anyone's feelings. That's not what it's about. For me, it's not what I'm experiencing, it's what your writings mean for public policy. That's what concerns me. And that's not just about my daughter.[14]

Peter Singer and Jeff McMahan have teamed up to defend the rights of animals at the expense of some people. Using intelligence as the criteria for moral significance, they attempt to illustrate how chimps or pigs (being more intelligent than some individuals) have more worth. It is this argument that forms the basis of their advocacy to stop animal testing, the eating of meat and a host of other reasons that humans have to kill animals. Most worrying about McMahan's comments in this remarkable exchange is: "The question is what is it about people like your daughter that makes moral demands on other people that nonhuman animals can make on any of us." In other words, why should anyone care about or help pay to support the life of someone like Kittay's daughter, Sesha? As with most deeply disturbing conversations, Kittay has found the words to illuminate her argument only afterwards. "I now see how I must reply," she wrote recently. She reminds us that Singer and McMahan acknowledged the special relationship that Kittay has with her daughter and that that relationship is more morally significant than any relationship she could have with an animal. In this concession, Singer and McMahan have ascribed personhood to Sesha. The care of children in our society is not simply a private matter — we have laws and policies that ensure there is a public duty to fund their good upbringing. The moral significance of the mother/child relationship is greater than the significance of our relationship to animals. "It takes a village to raise a child" takes on political meaning here. If Kittay is right, and

I believe she is, looking after our most vulnerable citizens really IS a public concern. And we should care about this exchange of views, because the ideas of ethicists, even expressed in the faraway and rarefied settings of Ivy League universities, have a way of ending up in our own hearts and minds when we are asked about the rights and wrongs of difficult questions.

CHAPTER SEVEN

Worthy of Dignity

If she ever met him, I wonder what the American philosopher Martha Nussbaum would make of Nicholas. I
wonder if she would see him as worthy of sympathy, but
not respect.

When Nussbaum began to work with Sen on
Capability matters, she decided that Sen's ideas needed
fleshing out for the real world. So, she devised a list of ten
essential capabilities that, if reached to a minimum level,
constituted the ingredients of a decent life — a life worth
living. Nussbaum calls these minimum core social entitle-
ments for a decent life the "Central Human Capabilities."

1. **Life.** Being able to live to the end of a human life of normal
    length; not dying prematurely, or before one's life is so
    reduced as to be not worth living.
2. **Bodily Health.** Being able to have good health, including
    reproductive health; to be adequately nourished; to have
    adequate shelter.
3. **Bodily Integrity.** Being able to move freely from place to
    place; to be secure against violent assault, including sexual

assault and domestic violence, having opportunities for
sexual satisfaction and for choice matters of reproduction.

4. **Senses, Imagination and Thought.** Being able to use the
senses, to imagine, think, and reason — and to do these
things in a "truly human" way, a way informed and cul-
tivated by an adequate education, including, but by no
means limited to, literacy and basic mathematical and scientific training. Being able to use imagination and thought
in connection with experiencing and producing works and
events of one's own choice, religious, literary, musical, and
so forth. Being able to use one's mind in ways protected
by guarantees of freedom of expression with respect to
both political and artistic speech, and freedom of religious
exercise. Being able to have pleasurable experiences and
to avoid nonbeneficial pain.

5. **Emotions.** Being able to have attachments to things and
people outside ourselves; to love those who love and
care for us, to grieve at their absence; in general, to love,
to grieve, to experience longing, gratitude and justified
anger. Not having one's emotional development blighted
by fear and anxiety. (Supporting this capability means supporting forms of human association that can be shown to
be crucial in their development.)

6. **Practical Reason.** Being able to form a conception of the
good and to engage in critical reflection about the planning of one's life. (This entails protection for the liberty of
conscience and religious observance.)

7. **Affiliation.**
A. Being able to live with and toward others, to recognize
and show concern for other human beings, to engage in

various forms of social interaction; to be able to imagine the situation of another. (Protecting this capability means protecting institutions that constitute and nourish such forms of affiliation, and also protecting the freedom of assembly and political speech.)

B. Having the social bases of self-respect and nonhumiliation; being able to be treated as a dignified being whose worth is equal to that of others. This entails provisions of nondiscrimination on the basis of race, sex, sexual orientation, ethnicity, case, religion, national origin.

8. **Other Species.** Being able to live with concern for and in relation to animals, plants and the world of nature.

9. **Play.** Being able to laugh, to play, to enjoy recreational activities.

10. **Control Over One's Environment.**

A. **Political.** Being able to participate effectively in political choices that govern one's life; having the right of political participation, protections of free speech and association.

B. **Material.** Being able to hold property (both land and movable goods), and having property rights on an equal basis with others; having the right to seek employment on an equal basis with others; having the freedom from unwarranted search and seizure. In work, being able to work as a human being, exercising practical reason and entering into meaningful relationships of mutual recognition with other workers.[15]

A cursory reading of the list reveals the simple fact that Nussbaum did not consider people with disabilities in her thinking. But she is a great philosopher and although she recognizes that people with disabilities may very well never be capable of attaining the minimum standard of functioning, Nussbaum recognizes that this poses a philosophical problem of their right to be. If practical reasoning is at the heart of being human, where does this leave our sons and daughters with cognitive disabilities? People like Eva Kittay's daughter Sesha have been persecuted, shunned or even murdered; indeed, inclusion and equality are very contemporary concepts. Disability activists have criticized Nussbaum's early work that positions people with severe cognitive disabilities outside an ethical framework for freedom and fairness that works for everyone else. But her more recent work shows a change of heart. In *Frontiers of Justice*, Nussbaum attempts to reconcile her list of ten basic capabilities (that she developed as a response to Sen's approach, which is far less prescriptive) with a theory of justice for people with severe disabilities.[16]

As examples, she uses the lives of three young people: her own nephew, Arthur, who has Asperger and Tourette syndromes; philosopher Eva Feder Kittay's daughter, Sesha, who has cerebral palsy and a severe cognitive delay; and the writer and intellectual Michael Berube's son, Jamie, who has Down syndrome. She describes the personalities, talents and abilities of these three young people and concludes that they may never become functionally able to repay society for the resources that they consume. If society provided the appropriately assistive training and supports to Arthur and Jamie, they might eventually be employed. However, Sesha is more limited in the range of her potential productive contribution to society, even with increased support. Nussbaum examines whether Sesha is "a different form of life altogether, or do we say that she will never be able to have a flourishing human life, despite our best efforts."[17] Nussbaum concludes that in a just society, Sesha would not have been born with disabilities; scientific advancements would have removed her handicaps. So, Sesha is excluded from Martha Nussbaum's Capability Approach because she will never attain adequate functional ability to be "human."

Kittay may be a great philosopher, but she is also a mother. She retaliates by describing her daughter's life as "richly human and full of dignity." She continues: "We need to work hard to see that her life is not tragic."[18] Over the years, I have met many other parents of children with disabilities. Not one of these parents sees their child as tragic or would wish them to be seen as such. Nicholas, Sesha, Jamie and Arthur are adored for being their essential selves. They are celebrated for living their lives richly in the face of daily struggles. This is not tragic; it is a call for understanding about the role of love in families and the need for community support.

CHAPTER EIGHT

Some Mother's Child

A friend who is a priest in the Church of England once remarked that "God's gift to us is being. Our gift to God is becoming." This idea rings true in the context of Reinders', Pailin's and Kittay's ideas. The essential worth of another is received love: God's love, a mother's love, a father's love, a sibling's love — it doesn't matter. This love is the great equalizer. It is the core of our humanity and our humaneness. It is no coincidence that the worst insults in most languages are against one's mother. The fundamental insult is not against an individual's mother per se, but against the idea of received love from someone whose love is unequivocal. An insult against one's mother can be interpreted as completely dehumanizing — that this person is not worth loving, such that his essential relationship of love and basic trust can be made dirty and worthless.

There is a sense of inertia associated with the idea of being, whereas action is linked to becoming. In being, there are no expectations of doing because the key is receiving love, not giving it. In becoming, there is implied potential, action and choice. It is within this space that human flourishing depends on freedom to exercise abilities, which is why Sen's ideas are so fundamental to understanding how people living in circumstances of deprivation can better their lives. But it is in this sense of being and receiving love that we experience being fully human. If we accept this idea of being as right and true, and if we accept that human flourishing requires freedom to exercise capability in order to reach individual potential, we can begin to think about a system of fairness and equality that includes everyone, even those who lack capacity for reason or purposive action.

A few years ago, I happened upon the obituary of a woman who had had many children and grandchildren. I recall being struck by the words, written by a grandchild and suffused with love: "Although there were so many in our family, she made each of us feel known and loved." In knowing and loving someone, there is a suggestion of unconditional acceptance made personal, and a steadfast loyalty. This woman must have been a wonderful listener. To me, this is a description of an ideal mother or grandmother.

To understand how this understanding of mothers' love must inform our compassionate acts, it is important to look at how to care for those deemed least worthy of receiving that love. Helen Prejean, the nun depicted in the book and film *Dead Man Walking*, is one example of offering the most challenging compassion. Even our worst criminals are "some mother's son." Nothing in this story suggests that crimes committed by these men should not be punishable by society and the law. But there is a clear recognition that human contact with at least one compassionate listener is important even for the most hardened criminals who are facing the death penalty.

Closer to home, I recall one story told to me by Vickie Cammack at PLAN. An elderly woman approached staff at PLAN in Vancouver with a difficult request. Her only daughter had received a life sentence in a forensic psychiatric facility and had already served some years. The elderly mother feared that with her own passing, her daughter would never have another visitor. The woman asked whether PLAN could find someone to visit her daughter and bring her favourite chocolate chip cookies once a month. The staff at PLAN agreed to try and a paid facilitator or "community connector" visited the daughter in prison once a month for one hour. Eleven monthly visits passed with not one word exchanged between the two women. The daughter refused to speak or acknowledge the facilitator at all. At the end of a year and on her twelfth visit, the facilitator said to the prisoner, "Your mum has asked me to visit you because she is worried that she is dying soon. After your mum dies, it's possible you will never have another visitor. Today is my last visit with you, because I agreed with your mum that I would try for a year to help you. What would you like me to do next month?" The woman looked up from her lap for the first time in eleven months and said, "You can do what you want." The PLAN facilitator arrived at the prison the next month with chocolate chip cookies. During their months of silence, the facilitator had passed the time by knitting. Eventually, the facilitator taught the prisoner to knit. In this special case, the facilitator dropped her paid role and rather than introducing her to an unpaid friend, became the prisoner's friend herself. I recall telling this story to the board of directors at Lifetime Networks Ottawa, a PLAN affiliate organization that I helped to found. One of the directors was dismissive, remarking, "Well, if you go around saying that our charity helps murderers who are insane, we are never going to get any support in this town!" I believe that he missed the point.

The point of the story is the notion that the mother–daughter relationship is sacred to civil society. We must not allow anyone to be found unworthy of at least one caring relationship — even those who by all appearances do not deserve a speck of human kindness. Central to this understanding is that one-half of that particular relationship was a mother who was beside herself with grief and worry. PLAN trumpets safety and security through caring relationships. But this safety and security is for all who choose it, not just some.

Amartya Sen intentionally coined the term Capability *Approach* and not Capability *Theory*, to allow for maximum flexibility in applying his thinking about human freedom. In the context of my family, I wanted to examine the extent to which we have enjoyed the "freedom to be" — an existence measured against a myriad of choices that other families take for granted.

By "being," I mean participation in community life

and public institutions for my family. It also implies acceptance in those spheres. But participation in community life is not easy or straightforward. Like all families, individual needs may pit themselves against the freedoms of another.

In order for Nicholas to have the freedom to pursue a life that he values, he must have twenty-four-hour nursing care. For many years, I performed that care myself. Now we have a team of paid staff around the clock. They allow Nicholas to pursue his interests and live a good life, but they also permit me to flourish as well. The help that we have now that Nicholas is twenty-one can be seen as reciprocity from the state to me, for having performed the first eighteen years of Nicholas' care.

During Nicholas' younger years, there was no one in my family who could have taken over my responsibilities, and I became worn out. We always relied on Jim's work to sustain us, and in order for him to flourish in his career, he had to be unimpeded by the constraints of carrying out Nick's physical care. Our Natalie's freedom involved carving out a space for herself in the family, one that excluded her brother, whose needs, she felt (with some reason), always trumped her own. Balancing these fundamental but conflicting freedoms on behalf of my family has been my life's work. And what of my own freedoms? How can a mother possibly demand a freedom to "be" in the face of so many competing interests? If looking at personal reality is like looking through a prism, perhaps I needed to turn the glass a little to capture a different view. Perhaps I needed to imagine a new set of preconditions for freedom.

CHAPTER NINE

Welcome to Holland

"So Brother Matthew locked the gate behind me, and I was enclosed in the four walls of my new freedom."
— *Thomas Merton,* The Seven Storey Mountain, *1948*

Over the years, I learned not to define my freedom to "be" as having anything to do with choice as an engine for happiness in my life. Besides, my own self-interest was so tied to the interests of my children that my sense of personal freedom to change was something of the past. When other mothers in my neighbourhood began to work part-time or took courses as their children grew, I began to work at accepting the inevitability of my unchanging role. Nick's physical care was always going to be similar to that of a newborn. He required total care and always would. Any idea of exercising personal choice as a measure of my own self-worth had to die.

In 1996, we left England and returned to Ottawa. It was late August when we moved back into our house surrounded by a large lawn on two levels. Tall pine trees shaded the roof, and a mature hedge bordered the street in front and on the side, stretching around the corner. "The grass looks dead over there," I said to Jim. He went over to investigate and, meaning to pluck out a few blades, found the turf lifting in his hand like a rug off the floor. It was an infestation of grubs that were attacking lawns throughout the city, consuming the roots of grass at an enormous rate. The first year we tried sprays and treatments, and the second year, when they came back, I decided to plant a garden. In a small section, I ripped up the dead grass, spread topsoil and spent hours searching garden nurseries for plants that could withstand both shade and the acidity of pine needles on the ground. I planted Japanese spurge around the base of the trees, as well as hostas, euonymus, ferns and tulip bulbs for the spring. I planted peonies where the late afternoon sun would shine. I was learning to be alone.

The following spring, a house on the next street was being bulldozed to make room for a new mansion to be constructed. I asked a member of the demolition team about the plants in the garden — would they be saved? "No, ma'am, the whole property'll be bulldozed tomorrow." I ran home for plant pots and a spade. I threw them into the back of our van and drove around the corner ready to rescue as many plant orphans as I could carry. This was a mature perennial garden, planted and tended carefully over many years. A bank of day lilies bordered the back wall of the empty house. A wide circular bed held bearded irises, tulips, daffodils and a good-sized rhododendron. Ferns blanketed the ground under a gigantic maple tree.

I felt so bittersweet peering into the house where children had been raised, holidays had been celebrated, families had argued. Tomorrow there would be nothing left to hold these memories and experiences. I dug as many plants as I could, filled the van three times over, and began the backbreaking digging to get every bush and flower into the ground before Nicholas came home from school at 3 p.m. So began my love affair with growing things. At first, some new plants died almost immediately. I began to pay more attention to the little cards in the pots at the garden centre, reading each carefully. I realized they were serious when they said "full sun." For three years, my garden was my refuge. In the first days of spring, I would step into the half-frozen earth, scanning the ground for any green shoots. Even if they weren't there in the morning, sometimes they would appear by the afternoon if the day was particularly warm.

I remember reading a film review in the newspaper. I never actually saw the film and I cannot even recall its name. But the reviewer's words are still with me today. The film was about a convent somewhere in Europe. A young nun complained about having to wash dishes and scrub pots. The Mother Superior chastised her, saying, "There is meaning in those dishes, in the act of scrubbing." As the reviewer said, the film was a testament to the idea that the extraordinary exists within the ordinary; that the entire moral universe can be found in the mundane tasks of everyday life. This sense of wholeness and connectedness is what I found in my garden.

Outside our front door in Ottawa, we had a black wrought-iron openwork light fixture. Each spring, a pair of tiny sparrowlike birds called redpolls came to nest in our lamp. The first year they came, all their bits of straw and string simply fell through the mesh onto the ground. Annoyed by the mess, we swept up and thought nothing more of it until one day, there on the ground lay two tiny, broken bright blue eggs. I wept a little, berating myself for not understanding their simple need to have a safe nest for their offspring.

The next year when we heard their distinctive chirps at the door, Jim cut some bits of cedar and created a floor on the base of the lamp. Nest building began in earnest, and soon there were four tiny eggs tucked up amongst downy roan feathers. That year, I watched as the mum kept her eggs warm and the father worried nearby. They eventually hatched into a noisy quartet of open beaks and soon enough they were ready to fly. I sat an entire day, watching in suspenseful anticipation as every redpoll in the area arrived on our pine tree to begin "training" with the youngsters. By turns, each bird would fly to the top of the lamp, perch there for a second and fly off to the nearby branch. The young birds had a tricky rite of passage: they had to fly inside the lamp and exit through a narrow passage at the top of the ironwork. By dusk, all the birds had left the nest and we could finally turn on the light and resume our life without our temporary tenants.

These birds living in my midst, nurtured by us and by the rest of the flock, gave me a certain antidote against loneliness. I had genuine curiosity about the life in my garden and most certainly, felt "some minute, divine spark inside me." By this time I had given up on any idea of justice or natural order in the world. Contained in my garden, I thought, there is transcendence; there is grace. I began to think that peeling potatoes, raking leaves and mixing cakes were all a sort of prayer. I began to understand that to be free, I had to have an antidote to despair.

Theodore Zeldin writes about how some people have acquired immunity to loneliness in his book *An Intimate History of Humanity*.[19] In fact, one of his themes is actually called "Loneliness as an Obstacle to Freedom," which of course speaks directly to me, given that I am discussing my family's "Freedom to Be." Being the mother of a child with multiple disabilities is, by definition, a very lonely life. Nicholas' illness, mobility challenges and communication difficulties never made us top of the guest list at friends' and neighbours' homes. When his health deteriorated and pain became our constant enemy, we hardly ever spoke to anyone save health professionals. I had wonderful friends and an extraordinarily supportive family, but I found it impossible to share the gut-wrenching worry that seemed so exclusive to our little family. Zeldin talks about the fear of loneliness as being a great barrier to personal freedom. He observes that those who have overcome a fear of loneliness have done so through experiencing a solitary lifestyle, whether by choice or even by incarceration. But he also says, "The final form of immunisation has been achieved by thinking that the world is not just a vast, frightening wilderness, that some kind of order is discernible in it, and that the individual, however insignificant, contains echoes of that coherence. People who believe in some supernatural power have their loneliness mitigated by the sense that, despite all the misfortunes that overwhelm them, there is some minute divine spark inside them."

Apparently I am not alone in my experience. In Reinders' book, he quotes another mother of a son with multiple and severe disabilities:

> For many, many years, I was confined to the house, alone and without the support of relatives or friends. My husband was at work all day and I was with Oliver and the other five children. This enforced seclusion was difficult for me; I had a restless, seeking spirit. Through Oliver I was held still. I was forced to embrace a silence and solitude where I could "prepare the way of the Lord." Sorrow opened my heart and I "died." I underwent this "death" unaware that it was a trial by fire from which I would rise renewed — more powerfully, more consciously alive.[20]

Reinders astutely points out that "what she expresses and affirms is not a life that has the choosing self as its object. The choosing self is precisely what in her view had to die in order for the new self to rise from its ashes like a phoenix."[21]

It is a strange paradox that in order to be free, the mother of a child with severe disabilities in our society has to relinquish the choosing self. I can remember thinking more than once, "Okay, I give up. I give up on imagining that I have a life. I am a servant, not a master. I will be still. I will watch and listen as I wait for Nicholas' next crisis."

It is ironic and paradoxical that the key to surviving the experience of caring for someone as dependent as my son means giving up on freedom of choice. The capabilities of my family cannot be measured on the same scale as others — it is part of our job as people who love someone who is very dependent to redefine happiness and achievement.

Every parent of a newly diagnosed child with a disabling condition will undoubtedly be handed a parable by Emily Perl Kingsley. Kingsley began her career as a writer for the children's television show *Sesame Street* in 1970. In 1974, she gave birth to a son, Jason, with Down syndrome, and it was her experience that led her to write "Welcome to Holland":

I am often asked to describe the experience of raising a child with a disability — to try to help people who have not shared that unique experience to understand it, to imagine how it would feel. It's like this…

When you're going to have a baby, it's like planning a fabulous vacation trip — to Italy. You buy a bunch of guide books and make your wonderful plans. The Coliseum. The Michelangelo David. The gondolas in Venice. You may learn some handy phrases in Italian. It's all very exciting.

After months of eager anticipation, the day finally arrives.

You pack your bags and off you go. Several hours later, the plane lands. The stewardess comes in and says, "Welcome to Holland."

"Holland?!?" you say. "What do you mean Holland?? I signed up for Italy! I'm supposed to be in Italy. All my life I've dreamed of going to Italy."

But there's been a change in the flight plan. They've landed in Holland and there you must stay.

The important thing is that they haven't taken you to a horrible, disgusting, filthy place, full of pestilence, famine and disease. It's just a different place.

So you must go out and buy new guide books. And you must learn a whole new language. And you will meet a whole new group of people you would never have met.

It's just a different place. It's slower-paced than Italy, less flashy than Italy. But after you've been there for a while and you catch your breath, you look around…and you begin to notice that Holland has windmills…and Holland has tulips. Holland even has Rembrandts.

But everyone you know is busy coming and going from Italy…and they're all bragging about what a wonderful time they had there. And for the rest of your life, you will say, "Yes, that's where I was supposed to go. That's what I had planned."

And the pain of that will never, ever, ever, ever go away… because the loss of that dream is a very very significant loss.

But…if you spend your life mourning the fact that you didn't get to Italy, you may never be free to enjoy the very special, the very lovely things…about Holland.[22]

I believe that Amartya Sen's challenge is for all those in Holland to find value there and for all those in Italy to value Holland's goodness. If we accept that diversity is a good thing, then we must break down borders between those two "countries." No one should live without knowing Rembrandt.

CHAPTER TEN

Nicholas and Capability

Every mother can imagine being her child. In a sense, this is what loving mothering is made of — a constant imagining of being her child. A mother puts a sweater on her child because *she* feels cold.

As Eva Kittay said: "I propose that being a person means having the capacity to be in certain relationships with other persons, to sustain contact with other persons, to shape one's own world and the world of others, and to have a life that another person can conceive of as an imaginative possibility for him or herself. It is a definition that brings our relationships (real and imaginative) with others to the centre of any conception of personhood."[23]

So, let me set the stage for imagining Nicholas in his full and glorious humanity. I will begin by describing what possibilities in his life circumstances he requires in order to be fully human. Generally speaking, there is a tacit understanding in our family of an expectation that we can and should do something constructive and positive with the circumstances of our lives. Our challenge is to convert the disability experience into something we call a good life. In this department, Nicholas leads the charge.

The Capability Approach gives us a framework for understanding how this conversion might occur, even against all odds. Nicholas has two central capabilities aside from those he shares with his able-bodied peers. The first capability is to be free from pain. I would argue that a great many people with long-term care conditions, including the elderly, share this capability with Nicholas. Pain is a messy, frantic business. Like extreme poverty and illness, it has the capacity to cause great misery. As such, I will call it an injustice. When someone is in extreme pain, everyone tries to help. Individuals and state services become involved as everyone weighs in with possible solutions. Our family's efforts to control Nicholas' pain with the assistance of health and social care authorities reveal how the Capability Approach applied individually and collectively provides some sensible mapping clues for others in a similar situation. Sen maintains that justice can be achieved by removing injustices, one at a time. I have said that for Nicholas, pain is an injustice. But our experience of trying to alleviate his pain sometimes caused other injustices. Now, we have finally achieved a relatively pain-free lifestyle for Nicholas — one that is very reduced, and yet very rich.

The other capability I wish to explore is Nicholas' ability to pursue his activities of life "as if" he did not have a disability; that is not to say that Nick thinks he can achieve the same functional goals as his peers — it is more about how others speak to him and see him in the course of his day. Nicholas has a strong "stick on the ice, elbows up" kind of male ego. The self he presents to the world is tough, funny and completely unsentimental. Sometimes new people will meet him and mistake his smile for sweetness or worse, simple-mindedness. For Nicholas, balancing good manners while putting people straight is challenging, and it often falls to friends and family to keep his ego intact.

To understand both these capabilities and how they apply to Nicholas, it is vital to know about Nick's personality and his closest relationships. Last year, Jim and I were invited to the opening of an art exhibition at the National Gallery in London. Tim Gardner, a young Canadian watercolourist, had spent the year there as artist in residence. A collection of thirty or so paintings, the result of studying the gallery's permanent collection for inspiration, was on display. We entered the grand hall and were directed towards an archway leading to a smaller room where the sounds of people talking softly and glasses clinking could be heard. Groups of people parted to reveal a large painting on the wall opposite me. It was a portrait of Tim's brother, but I did not know that then. In the style of magic realism, it was his brother's angular face in profile. The background was a prairie landscape, empty except for earth, grass and sky. His eyes squinting into the distance, this boy seemed to be saying, "I am strong, I am a survivor. Look out there, not at me. Look where I am going, look with me." I felt I was looking at Nicholas. I drew up to the painting — I wanted so badly to touch his cheek — this young man who seemed so proud yet so fragile and alone in that landscape. All at once, I realized that my cheeks were wet, so I gathered myself and moved to look at the next image — this one of mountains and sky.

Recently, I came across a story that Nick had written in elementary school. It illuminates his resilience, determination and positive outlook that has sustained him from a very young age. The story is called "Cameron the Race Car Driver."

Once upon a time, there was a man named Cameron. He was a race car driver for Fisher-Price. He raced with his dad who was also a race car driver. On the weekend, he worked as a handicap bus driver. Cameron was a crazy driver, but not with the handi-bus. One race, Cameron got into a terrible accident and wrecked his car and got hurt. Cameron had to go to the hospital. Afterwards, he went back home to try and get better. He was in pain from head to his toes. He had to stay at home for nine years. After that, Cameron trained very hard to get back into shape. He wore a red t-shirt and running shoes. He wanted to be a race car driver very badly. For some reason, Cameron stopped training and decided to walk around the world. He did it six times. Now that Cameron was back from his travelling, he could be a race car driver again. But, he had to start from the beginning. He had to learn to ride a tricycle, then a bike, then he rode in a buggy, then in a tiny car. As he got better, he could drive his racing car again. His first race back was the British

Grand Prix. He started at the pole position. But Cameron slipped on a banana peel at the start and spun out of control into another car. He was not hurt this time! After this race, Cameron wanted to win the next one in Argentina and he did! Cameron went on to win the driver championship for the next three years. When he retired from car racing, Cameron drove the handi-bus again. The end.

Nowadays, Nicholas does not like to be reminded of his old school stories. He does not care for any evidence of his younger, more innocent self. And Nick will not look at photos of himself. He will become very upset and angry if someone even jokingly plays home movies, confronting him with a younger version of himself. Sure, there were times when I said, "Nicholas, adjust your expectations. Look at yourself. You have a disability." But mostly, Jim and I have plunged headlong into adapted skiing, neighbourhood ice hockey, ball hockey with the local boys' and girls' club, and endless train rides during his boyhood locomotive obsession. Speed and danger were Nick's definition of fun, so we adapted waterskiing for him by tying the windsurf board to our ski boat at the cottage. Nick would sit on a cushion between the legs of his helper and laugh hysterically when his helper shouted "Gun it!" During all of these family activities, we always expected Nicholas to cope with the same scrapes and tumbles as his sister. More than that, we used these activities to tease Nick, ensuring that his ego never inflated and that he understood his place in the world as equal, not apart.

That said, Nicholas had and still has oodles of charm and he'll use it shamelessly to get any number of treats. But no treat is so coveted that he will accept it from someone who pities or babies him.

Halfway through grade ten and after much practice, Nick learned to say the "F" word. He splutters "Fffffuh, Ffffuh" and he'll pump up the volume if anyone dares kiss his cheek uninvited. The protection of his male pride is an unspoken imperative amongst our family and friends. Newcomers who break this rule are greeted with a loud "Ffffuh!"

Nicholas believes that not acknowledging his disability means not giving in to it. He believes that if he does not gaze at his own image he will be just like any other young man — a pair of eyes looking out for speed, danger and shenanigans.

A few years ago, Nicholas was lying on a stretcher outside the operating room at the Children's Hospital of Eastern Ontario. As I stood by his bedside waiting for him to be called for surgery, I knew he was afraid. For a while, we watched other parents as they handed their child or baby to a kind nurse or doctor in scrubs. As each baby was whisked away over the shoulder of a surgeon, parents would stand waving and smiling until the door shut. To cheer Nick up, I began to wonder aloud which parents would cry when the O.R. doors shut. Pretty soon, we were placing bets and trying to stifle our giggles. I told the nurse who arrived for Nicholas about our game. "Oh Nick, you're terrible!" she cried. "Yeah!" he said proudly as he glided through the doors and down the corridor, fist-punching the air.

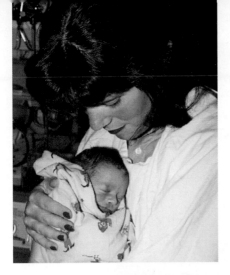

Cuddling Nicholas at
the maternity hospital

Nicholas trying to digest
organized religion

Amanda, our Golden
Retriever, performing
infant stimulation
exercises with Nick

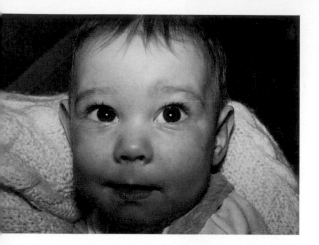

To me, Nicholas looked "normal" and beautiful

Nicholas, age one year, with Dad at the cottage

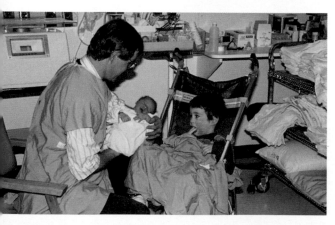

Nick greeting his newborn sister, Natalie, for the first time

Age one year, at the
cottage with Nana
Wright, summer 1989

I nicknamed him "Bunnybear"
as a nod to his Jekyll and Hyde
personality. For his first birthday, I made two cakes, one a
bunny, the other a bear. Aunt
Karen is holding the bear cake.

Nicholas with
Grandma Thomson
at Christmas, 1991

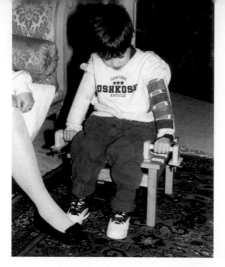

Nick working hard to sit
in Conductive Education
· lesson, 1993

In London, age seven, 1995

With Natalie and
friend Josh cooking
at home, 1995

Nicholas' first ever bus ride
on public transportation,
with former after-school
helper and lifelong pal
John Bilder, 1997

Christmas 1997
with Uncle Frank
and Dad

With friends at the Disabled
Ski Association Awards
Banquet, 1998

Skiing with Dad

Learning to love lobster
in Kennebunk, Maine,
with John Bilder in 1998

Elementary school,
Grade 6 graduating
class, Churchill
Alternative School,
Ottawa, June 2000

Nicholas learning how to play computer games using a single switch

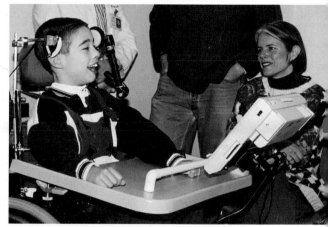

Nick learning how to use head switches to control a speech computer

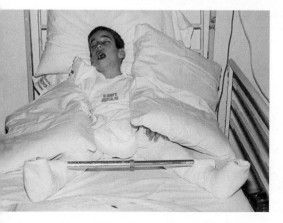

The first of many hip surgeries, this one in London, 1995

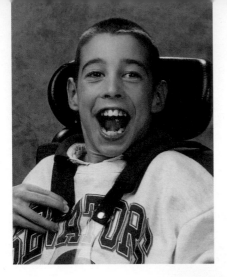

Nicholas' Grade 4 school photo, in Ottawa

On the beach at the cottage with our dog Amanda, Auntie Cathie, Uncle Gerry and cousin Olivia

Nicholas, Natalie, Stone Cold Steve Austin and Jeremy, a friend who accompanied us on the trip

But keeping this pretense of bravado through wit and irony is no laughing matter. The alternative was, and is, too awful to contemplate. There have been only a few times that I have had to drop the jocular air and deal with some urgent truth. One such occasion was in 1991. Nicholas had been suffering from a vomiting bug and was hospitalized because of dehydration. An x-ray of his abdomen revealed that part of his stomach had herniated bubble-like, above the diaphragm. The doctors feared strangulation of this wayward part of his stomach and so ordered surgery. I sat on Nick's bed and began to describe my conversation with the doctor. Nick arched backwards and began to cry out "No! No!" I ordered him to listen and when he quietened, I said softly, "They say if you don't have this operation, you might die." There was silence in the room. "Okay," he said, hardly above a whisper. Then he changed the subject and began to tell me about a night nurse who sang to him in Polish.

Sesha, the daughter of Eva Feder Kittay, is a young woman with severe and multiple disabilities. Fed up with philosophical theories of dignity and human worth that excluded her daughter, Kittay attacks the idea of setting standards for what is *normal*.[24] She maintains that love and care are more deeply bound to dignity than the ability to think and reason, and I agree with her.

As a mother, Kittay sees the dignity of her daughter as rooted in her own relationship of love and care, but she calls for Sesha's dignity as a moral imperative for society as well.

So, I have a lot in common with Eva Kittay. I have the moral capacity to care for Nicholas and, many times, that care has entailed a careful effort to present Nicholas to the world as I see him: a whole, wonderful young boy with exceptional needs. For this reason, I have overspent on the latest fashions for him, ensured that his hair was styled, his teeth perfect and his tube feeds invisible.

At the same time, I have to see Nicholas as others see him, because if I didn't, I would not be able to make those fine adjustments necessary to ensure his dignity remains intact. That said, there have been times when, as if seeing him through a prism, the light shifted and I suddenly looked upon him the way a stranger would. Momentarily shamed by my betrayal, I would give my boy a kiss and remove myself to reconfigure my thoughts about his normalcy. Sometimes those moments occur when I allow myself to imagine Nicholas without disability. This is a dangerous path for a mother to tread. Caring alone at home for a child who is very different from his peers, it was easy enough to see beauty, delight and pure love. But out in public, suddenly noticing the stare of a passerby and looking again at Nick, there were moments that caught me by surprise.

In early 1996, we were living in London and I received a call from a crime writer who was married to a colleague of Jim's. She was writing a book about a boy who had no speech, yet had witnessed a murder. For her research, she asked to meet with me and Nicholas to see how we conversed without words. I agreed immediately and a week later when she arrived, we all walked to the park, Nicholas in his lightweight pushchair. He was eight years old at the time. I told the writer about Nicholas' many abilities and described with pride his learning successes at school. Then Nick noticed a group of his schoolmates playing soccer and began to complain about wanting to join the game. Perhaps I was running harder than usual to demonstrate how Nicholas could "score a goal," but the wheel hit a rock in the ground, the chair tumbled sideways and I fell on top of my boy. Nick began to scream in fright, my knee was bleeding and the other boys stared momentarily, then ran off. The writer sat on the park bench quite horrified. She seemed to sense that I didn't want help getting up, but my face was burning and I was furious that I had let Nicholas down badly. Now she would think all that talk of his intelligence, his abilities in sports appreciation and model making were all lies — just a sad mother's pipe dreams. My knee healed, Nicholas forgot all about our tumble and I learned to be more careful and guarded in mediating our delicate relationship with strangers.

Now that Nick is twenty-one and a young man, he has more responsibility for managing his own relations with the world. This he does largely by isolating himself from it. When he says that he would prefer to pass on a live concert by his favourite rock band, he might offer the excuse that he feels sick or tired. He might worry that transport to the arena will cause pain in his bad hip. Any of these excuses could be true, but it is also a fact that Nick refuses most outings these days. Recently, Nick's carer Alvaro and his partner bought a puppy. Nicholas and Alvaro walk the dog in the park across the street. At first, Nick was amused but suspicious about strangers stopping to stroke the puppy and ask about it. "Why? Why?" Nicholas demanded to know why people were stopping to chat. I explained that it was not to express sympathy or curiosity about Nicholas — it really was about the puppy. After that, he became more enthusiastic about his outings with the dog.

When Nicholas was a small boy, it was my job to present him to the world, and actually, it was fairly easy to convince people of his adorable qualities. Now, as an adult, he knows that negotiating a relationship with strangers is largely his own responsibility. He is fully aware that the world of adults can be harshly judgemental, and that even though his mother calls him handsome, strangers in the park might only see a disabled man in a wheelchair. Over the past few years since Nicholas has been at home and out of high school, he maintains a dignified environment in his bedroom. Occasionally, he meets someone who will be invited in for a drink and chat. With a little help from his aides, Nick is quite successful at negotiating a safe and happy social encounter. Nicholas would tell anyone that his life was full, exciting and interesting. He does not wish that his disability didn't exist, because he doesn't admit to a disability. For Nicholas, it's a kind of ruse that he insists we all buy into as a matter of life and death. What is harder to deny is Nick's world of pain.

CHAPTER ELEVEN

The Prison of Pain

I don't remember exactly when the pain began, but two years ago, at a time when I thought Nicholas might not survive, I watched all our home videos. One, a film of his ninth birthday celebration at the cottage, showed him on our balcony surrounded by family, friends, hot dogs and torn-open gift boxes. Early that day, I had prepared hamburger patties for more than twenty guests and had left them on the kitchen counter ready for the grill. Jim had built a golf course of sorts on our back lawn, using ski poles tied with plastic grocery-bag flags sunk into buried lidless tin cans in the ground. We had eighteen such holes, each with amusing "hazards." Jim helped Nicholas deliver handwritten invitations that read "The Nicholas Wright Invitational Golf Tournament to be held at the Royal and Ancient Lake MacDonald Golf Club."

As the golf game neared its finish, I went upstairs to collect the hamburgers for the bar-b-q. They were nowhere in sight. The platter sat clean and empty on the counter. I suddenly had a terrible thought and knew in my heart that I was right — Goldie, our golden retriever, had eaten them. Twenty generous hamburger patties couldn't fit into the stomach of a normal dog, but I knew the capacities of our Goldie from previous experience. By now, the golfers had congregated on the patio, ready for their lunch. I announced that hot dogs would be served instead of burgers because of one very greedy dog having just eaten our lunch. At the same time, my brother-in-law Gerry with his video camera captured Goldie on the beach below belching up mounds of raw hamburger on the sand. Frank, my sister's husband, was on-screen suggesting that I should patty them up again since the meat was still fresh.

As I watched the scene unfold on the videotape, I laughed again as hard as I had the first time it played out. Nicholas was happy, excited and full of jokes. Suddenly, though, his face changed. His laugh turned to a look of shock. "There," I thought, "is pain." That startled look and holding of breath would appear sometimes, and gradually we began to see it happening more frequently. We discovered that Nick's right hip was the problem, and that we could make him more comfortable by standing behind him, grabbing hold under his arms and pulling his body up and backwards. This had the effect of positioning his lower back against the chair — the same as anyone adjusting their position to sit up straight.

In February 1998, an x-ray showed that Nicholas' hip was partially dislocated and the doctor explained that surgery to reconstruct his hip was required. He described how in the operating room he would take a piece of the pelvic bone and carve out a V-shaped shim. He would then break the top of the femur and position the shim in the space, finishing by fixing a metal plate with screws to secure the repair. This would angle the ball of the femur into the socket of the hip joint. I was told that a transfusion might be necessary and that I could donate my own blood, because we shared the same type. This I did and we waited for the surgery date to arrive. No one in our family had ever experienced an orthopaedic surgery before, so we didn't really know what to expect.

That year for Christmas, I had given Jim and myself a weekend away at a spa. I knew that we both needed some alone time, and Jim was extremely stressed by his job at the Department of Foreign Affairs as director of central, southern and eastern Europe. The war in Kosovo was raging, and Jim was heading up the diplomatic strategy, as well as giving daily press briefings. Often, someone from overseas would wake us in the middle of the night to convey urgent messages from the war zone. I wasn't sure if we would be able to take the weekend away because our city was blanketed in ice and many roads and hotels were closed. Eastern Canada had been declared a state of emergency just two weeks before — we had lost power in our home and been told by the emergency response team to relocate to a hotel in order to keep Nick safe and warm.

The city was slowly recovering from the catastrophic damage of the ice storm, and even though we had power at home, some homes still didn't, so I was surprised to learn that the small country hotel was open for business.

I ordered a massage and relaxing herbal bath for Jim. The hotel had once been a priory and still had an aura of contemplation to match the Catholic artifacts. It was surrounded by woods and faced a frozen lake — the setting was lovely. Nicholas' surgery was set for the Monday. At the hotel, I tried to shake the impending doom I felt during the nights, but I remember lying awake in that birch-panelled room with its crucifix above our bed. I reviewed scenarios of Nicholas' funeral; I played out scenes of him waking with screams of pain. I felt a sickening weight in my stomach.

It was agreed beforehand that Nicholas would go straight to the intensive care unit from the operating room because of his disability and we were told of all the possible complications that could ensue. Nick was still asleep when they wheeled him across the hall into the ICU. Jim and I sat by his bedside, waiting for him to wake up, but fearing that moment too. Nicholas' pain was being controlled by a morphine infusion dripping automatically into his IV. He had received one unit of my blood during the surgery, and as I sat stroking his arms I hoped my blood was filled with strength and love. That is what I had told Nick before the surgery in an effort to soothe his fear. I gently lay my hands on his chest and closed my eyes, trying to will healing energy into his body.

By evening, he was still asleep when Jim asked, "Are there *supposed* to be two morphine pumps running?" I dropped Nick's hand and ran to the nurse. I remember watching his face turn ashen when I told him. The anaesthetist managing the postoperative pain medications had switched from one morphine pump to another, and in her hurry to finish her shift, had forgotten to disconnect the first pump. Nicholas had been receiving double the prescribed dose of morphine for four hours. As Nicholas lay there, his breathing shallow and slow from the morphine, we prayed for him to live. Jim went home to get some sleep and I found a parent room usually reserved for those attending their sick babies in the neonatal unit. It was a windowless, dark room with a single sofa — there was a white sheet crumpled and discarded after someone's brief respite. I lay down and slept for a few hours. When I came back to the blazing lights of the ICU, the nurse told me that Nicholas had spiked a high fever and that a urine culture showed a severe urinary tract infection, probably caused by the catheter. They started Nicholas on an antibiotic and I continued to worry, because Nicholas had still not woken up from the surgery. He began to have frequent diarrhea, and C-dificil, the dreaded hospital superbug, was diagnosed. The strongest antibiotic was prescribed, and Nick continued to sleep. Days passed and even needle jabs did not wake him.

Almost ten days later, Nicholas had still not woken up and I was frantic, thinking that the morphine overdose had caused more brain damage. Finally, the neurologist was called and he peered at Nick, checking his pupils. "He's snowed. The level of his epilepsy medicine is probably too high. We'll test it." The medication level was more than five times higher than normal and this had been causing Nicholas to be so drugged. The doctors concluded that Nick must have reacted in an unpredictable way to the mixture of antibiotic and epilepsy medicines. Finally, my boy awoke and I knew that he was all right. He was crying and blowing kisses, asking to go home.

After six days on the regular ward, our discharge date arrived and we were told to await a transport ambulance that would deliver Nick to our house on a stretcher. Discharge papers were signed and we waited for the transport to arrive. And waited. Apparently the ambulance service was busy with more urgent cases than simple stretcher taxi bookings. I was told that it might be midnight before we arrived home. After six hours of waiting, I decided to take Nick home myself in our van. I moved the front seat as far back as I could, then reclined the seat to its maximum. I put pillows on the floor to create a resting place for Nick's lower legs and observed the result. It looked good and I thought Nicholas could be comfortable in the seat. I just needed help to lift him into the van without grazing his casted leg on the door frame. Any slight jar might be very painful. Staff on the ward refused to help move Nicholas to the van because the doctor had ordered ambulance transport (never mind that it did not appear). Luckily, I had a young male helper with me and between the two of us, we managed to get Nicholas home by early evening without any tears.

I had transformed our family room into Nick's home hospital. I had his hospital bed positioned in front of the television and had managed to coerce the homecare authorities into providing seven nights of nursing. Our helper stayed with Nick while I headed out to the twenty-four-hour pharmacy to collect prescriptions for liquid codeine and muscle relaxants to ease the postoperative spasms that are severe in children with cerebral palsy. The pharmacist had the painkiller in stock, but said that he would order the muscle relaxants and have them by the morning. I thought we could manage with just the painkiller and besides, I thought, I had no choice.

When I arrived home, Nicholas was screaming and in full body spasm. A young nurse had arrived and as I was trying to soothe Nick, she emptied a syringe of codeine into his feeding tube. I heard the front door open — it was Jim coming home from work. He asked the nurse to move her car so he could park his to one side in the driveway. Parking behind the nurse would have meant getting up at 6 a.m., the end of her shift, something Jim didn't want to do. The van was safely in the garage. That night, there was a severe weather warning for heavy snow — the wind had come up and the air outside was white already, the visibility poor.

Watching Nicholas writhe and scream was intolerable, so I decided to call the hospital surgical ward and request that they give me some muscle relaxant medicine to help us through the night. They agreed to leave some at the emergency room desk. I grabbed the car keys, jumped into the van, clicked open the electric garage door and reversed down the driveway. I crashed hard into something, I couldn't see what. Metal was twisted and I hardly dared look at the back of our van. There, in the middle of the driveway was a low white sports car, obscured in the snowstorm. It was the nurse's car. She had moved it to make room for Jim to park his Subaru on the right side of the drive. Shaking, I went back in to face the nurse and Jim. "I hit your car," I stated evenly. The nurse asked me to repeat what I said. "You'll have to pay" was her response. I told her to move her car as I brushed Jim aside and went back to the van. I drove slowly, gripping the steering wheel on the highway through the storm to reach the hospital. Finally, I got the vials of medicine and returned home to find Nick had fallen asleep, exhausted.

The surgery held for two years, until Nicholas' hip dislocated again.

I did not think that any nightmare could be worse than the bleak time after Nick's first hip surgery, but I was wrong. In 2003, when Nicholas began to show signs of pain again and the x-ray showed that his hip had begun to come out of the socket a second time, I asked our surgeon about treatment options. His response was that a second major repair was out of the question. A fused hip would either condemn him to a sitting position for the rest of his life, or a lying position. The only option, the surgeon advised, was removing the ball of the joint altogether. It sounded horrendous to me — akin to cutting off a limb. It seemed too violent. Another young lad called Shane who was paralyzed with spina bifida had gone through the procedure and he reported feeling better — his hip was pain free and because he didn't stand or walk, he didn't miss the ball of his joint at all.

Still, I felt a sense of dread. Nicholas' x-rays were sent off to the Shriner's Hospital in Montreal for a second opinion. The specialist orthopaedic surgeons there reported back their recommendation to go ahead with the operation. There was nothing else for it — Jim and I decided to go ahead with the surgery. Signing the consent form felt like giving permission for Nick's execution.

Nicholas came through the surgery all right. He did have a small bout of e-coli blood poisoning, but that was dealt with quite easily with antibiotics. The pain was tolerable and he was discharged to the Rotary Home, a respite facility for children with physical disabilities that did double duty as an inpatient rehab facility for the kids in our community. I stayed there with Nick by day and went home in time for dinner with Jim and Natalie. It all seemed relatively fine, especially compared to the events that followed the first surgery. Fine, that is, until the cast came off.

Our surgeon was away the day that Nick was scheduled for cast removal, and he had asked me if I preferred to wait until he returned to work the following day. I was feeling confident and hopeful, so I declined his offer and brought Nicholas to be seen by two younger doctors. They began to saw open the cast. About halfway down Nick's leg, he suddenly spasmed terribly and screamed. It was obvious that he was in agony. One of the doctors called for Valium, but it had no effect. Finally, they administered ketamine, a powerful anaesthetic, and admitted him to hospital. Later, I would learn that Nick's spasticity caused the femur to migrate upwards into the pelvic bone. Removing the cast triggered a spasm that caused the pain. The pain caused more spasm, which caused more pain. It was excruciating to witness; I can't begin to imagine what Nick must have felt.

Nicholas was given morphine and muscle relaxants until we were finally able to return home on a slow release version of the narcotic and a higher dose of the medication to prevent spasms. Slowly the surgical scar healed, but Nicholas was still in pain and much less active than he had been just a couple of years before. I still thought of him as part of the ski club (where he raced downhill in a sit-ski), as a keen pickup hockey player and as the sports reporter for his school newspaper.

I felt frantic, trying to convince everyone at the hospital that he was still capable of all these things. His active life couldn't be over, not yet. Our surgeon was kind and gentle, but he had exhausted all of his options and we were in deep trouble. We consulted the pediatric pain team and were given some other medications to try — this time powerful anti-inflammatories. One doctor on the team suggested that we try nerve blocks and I was keen to give them a go. In the operating room, we were told, Nicholas would be given a light sedation, and his major nerves that fed the hip would be isolated by probing with a tiny catheter emitting a small electrical charge. When the probe made contact with the nerve, Nick's muscle would twitch visibly and the doctor would know it was in the correct location. Then, he would inject the catheter with a small amount of drug to temporarily paralyze the nerve. The idea was twofold: to see if that was the nerve causing the pain, and also to investigate whether perhaps with a day or two of pain relief, the pain would disappear for good or at least return in a lesser form.

The doctor explained that sometimes by silencing the pain for a short period, the body and mind might "forget" how bad it was and a new, milder form of discomfort might return.

We tried many, many of these blocks on all the nerves feeding Nicholas' hip. Finally, it was decided to inject Nick's hip and spine with phenol to permanently kill the lumbar plexus, the femoral, obturator and sciatic nerves. I was warned that there was a small chance of a painful neuralgia resulting from these injections — a pain that could be worse than the pre-existing one. I ignored the warnings and signed the consent form eagerly, as I prayed for our boy to be the active, happy child he once was. The phenol killed the nerve roots but burnt and damaged the nerve branches extending into his right foot, causing permanent searing pain. Unwittingly, we had spiralled into a situation that was out of control.

By now, Nicholas was understandably phobic about doctors and hospitals. If he heard me speaking on the telephone about his pain or other medical issues, he would become very angry. Though nonverbal, I knew perfectly well what Nick was saying: "Get off the phone! Quit talking

about me! I'm not going to the hospital so just shut up!"
In the presence of others, especially medical professionals,
Nicholas used all of his energy to feign wellness. In the
safety of home, he stopped eating, he cried, he screamed,
he constantly asked for a sock to cover his painful foot, only
to have it removed and then put on again.

One evening, I looked at his foot and noticed that
it looked swollen, the skin a mottled purplish colour. I
began to fear that perhaps the blood flow had been cut
off for some reason…a blood clot perhaps? I decided to
rely on the kindness of neighbours. Alan, who lived at the
end of our street, was an internist at the adult hospital in
Ottawa. He knew Nick from our walks in the park and
his black lab Buddy was a friend of our golden retriever
Goldie. Alan came into Nick's room and peered at his
foot. He placed his hand around Nicholas' ankle, explaining that a good pulse there meant no blood clot. The
pulse was indeed strong, so I put that particular worry
out of my head. Still, it felt somehow more hopeless that
no blood clot meant no explanation and no excision of
whatever horrible poison was causing Nick so much pain.
We were caught in a vortex of agony and sleeplessness.

Lawrence Becker, an American moral philosopher who has
written extensively on disability, talks about the caregiver's
responsibility to support the conception of good in the
patient.[25] I felt driven to support the good in Nicholas by
not abandoning the hope of recapturing the person he was
before his pain. To do so, I felt, was a betrayal not only

of his future, but his entire person and his "being." Many drugs and treatments had been tried and failed. Now, doctors on the pain team advised me to "adjust his lifestyle." I took that to mean leaving him in bed where he was most comfortable. Nicholas was sixteen years old, and I could not accept that his life as we knew it was effectively over.

A second opinion at two specialist hospitals in Montreal was arranged. Perhaps they had seen another child with no hip joint and failed permanent nerve blocks. At the Shriner's Orthopaedic Hospital, a young, bearded doctor shook his head sadly at Nicholas as he tutted. I thought I hadn't heard him correctly when he said, "We no longer recommend these surgical procedures in cases like your son, with cerebral palsy." Only eight months before, this doctor's colleagues at his hospital had given the second opinion to remove the ball of Nicholas' hip joint, and now this doctor was saying that they no longer recommended this procedure? I was stunned. There was nothing they could do to help Nicholas now.

At the next hospital, the doctor nodded knowingly as I recounted our history. "Ah yes," he said, "we have children like your son who have had phenol blocks after hip surgeries living in our long term-care hospital here."

"How are they doing?" I asked.

"Not good" was his quiet reply.

We returned to Ottawa and I began to plan for an in-patient stay at another children's hospital in Montreal. Perhaps the chronic pain team there could offer up new eyes and new ideas.

CHAPTER TWELVE

The Injustice of Pain

By 2004, the situation was unmanageable at home. Nicholas screamed at night — Jim or I would get up every forty-five minutes or so to reposition him or to give him pain medication. Many times I called the hospital in the night, asking to speak with the pain doctor on call. In hospitals, pain management falls within the department of anaesthesia. Sometimes the anaesthetists "do pain" and sometimes they only practise their craft in operating rooms, putting patients to sleep safely. More than once, when I frantically called doctors on that team to say that I had given the maximum allowed dose of morphine, but that Nick was still in terrible distress, the response was "Sorry, I don't do pain."

Some months earlier, I had applied to a children's wish foundation for Nicholas. Nick was a great fan of professional wrestling, and his fondest wish was to meet Stone Cold Steve Austin of the WWE. One day, someone from the Sunshine Foundation called to say that Nicholas' name had come up and he was to be given his wish to meet his hero. The closest location to meet Stone Cold was at a performance in New Jersey. Nicholas was over the moon with excitement and I desperately wanted to give him some wonderful pleasure to counter his pain. But I worried about the travel and how he could cope with the journey. In the end, I decided to make the quick trip for the meeting with Stone Cold, together with Natalie and a helper for Nicholas. So, on March 15, 2004, we managed the short flight to Newark , picked up a rental wheelchair van at the airport and found our hotel. Nicholas was pale, but managing all right and was very excited. He rested awhile in bed before we walked across the street to the stadium where we were introduced to "Mr. Stone Cold" and other stars of the World Wrestling Entertainment. They were all gracious and generous with their offers of photos and merchandise. Nicholas and Natalie had prepared a large poster board by way of an invitation to visit our family at the cottage on a lake in the Quebec Laurentians. There were photos together with a note that read "Dear Stone Cold, you are invited to visit at the cottage where we go fishing, drink beer and smoke cigars with my dad and the boys. You would fit right in!" Stone Cold (Steve Williams) was delighted with his invitation and with our gift of maple syrup. After our visit with the WWE stars, we returned to the hotel where Nicholas had another lie-down and I asked him whether he wished to attend the show in the evening. He was trying very hard to enjoy his "wish come true" and he said yes, he wanted to attend the show. We went to half of the show, returned to the hotel and packed for an early morning flight to Montreal, where we would be admitted to the children's hospital there for pain assessment.

The next day, my sister Karen met us at the Montreal airport and soon we were admitted to the hospital. Nicholas was exhausted and in pain. When Nick is excited, his muscles stiffen — his legs extend and move as if he's cycling in air. His back arches and his grin is something to behold. Now he was paying the price for his trip of a lifetime. A morphine infusion pump was started and therapists were consulted. The narcotic caused Nicholas to be nauseated and he began to retch. The spasms of heaving caused even more pain, and suddenly I noticed that something looking like coffee grounds was coming out of his feeding tube. Blood! Nicholas was bleeding internally and the doctors were called. They started him on an IV of a strong antacid and eventually he settled. I wondered if this hell would ever end.

Several years earlier, on October 24, 1993, a Saskatchewan farmer called Robert Latimer murdered his daughter, Tracy. Tracy Latimer had very similar disabilities to Nicholas', including hip pain resulting from cerebral palsy. Robert Latimer, unable to witness Tracy's pain and suffering, lifted her into the front seat of his pickup truck and connected the exhaust pipe to the cab. Tracy died and the public's heart went out to her loving father. Robert Latimer was charged with second-degree murder and was eventually given the mandatory minimum sentence of ten years in jail. But the court of public opinion held differently. By January 1995, seven thousand Canadians had signed a petition to free Latimer and ten thousand more petitions were in circulation. By late November 1997, more than $100,000 had been raised in a legal defence fund. In a CBC Radio interview, Latimer famously commented, "I honestly don't believe there was ever any crime committed here."

Like me, Robert Latimer felt compelled to defend his child's capability to be pain free. Yet our parental perspectives on how to achieve this were light years apart. Recently, I had a conversation with a distinguished physician from the Harvard University medical centres. When I described to him all of the surgical procedures Nicholas has had and their sometimes disastrous results, he asked, "Don't you feel sometimes that you are torturing him?" The answer to that question is not straightforward. I felt on a mission to get back a life with Nicholas that we had once enjoyed — a life for him that meant fun, activity and inclusion in his school, his family and his community. I was determined not to give up on Nicholas and a future good life for him.

In hindsight, I know that I expected too much of doctors and hospitals. At each round of nerve blocks, I believed that Nicholas would wake up pain free. When the doctors explained that the blocks would "kill the nerves," I assumed that that meant Nicholas would be numb in his hip. When he experienced the jabs of pain that made him flinch when I lifted him out of his chair, I thought the procedure had failed. As ever, Nicholas was most comfortable lying in bed. Sitting in his wheelchair over long periods caused him great discomfort. Sitting through a class at school, for example, became impossible.

Because Nicholas still had pain, I kept begging the doctors to try other procedures. I wasn't ready to give up on an active future for Nicholas and I didn't understand that nerve blocks are only ever a partial fix. The doctors would enter Nick's hospital room where he would be lying still in bed, comfortable and smiling. When I complained again and again that Nicholas still had pain in sitting and especially when I lifted him out of bed, they could not or would not believe it. My credibility at the hospital plummeted to zero and a psychologist was called in to speak to Nicholas without me present. I was caught up in some vortex of misunderstanding and I knew that I was branded as difficult and possibly crazy by the only people who could help Nicholas. I felt desperate.

By 2005, Nick was spending most of his time learning from the bed in his high school's nursing room. Back in January 2001, I had written a letter to the editor of the Ottawa newspaper supporting the Supreme Court of Canada's ruling on Robert Latimer's sentence. I believe that the public would have reacted very differently if Tracy Latimer had been able-bodied, or if she had been suffering from the effects of cancer, for example. It seemed evident to me that because many people were repulsed by the awfulness of giving total care to someone as disabled as Tracy, they assuaged their guilt by supporting Robert Latimer — exalting him, even. People who supported Robert Latimer were so afraid of dependency that they were pleased to erase the evidence of it.

It's not that I don't question the pain and suffering I caused Nicholas by choosing major surgeries. I do. Many times, I was racked with guilt when he woke in the recovery room and I saw pain, pleading and panic in his eyes. But I am essentially an optimist. I always believed that we could do better, that Nicholas could beat his disability and that pure determination together with dogged research could win out over a stance of resignation. So it came as a great blow to me when each surgery, each intervention seemed to unleash some new horror. Applying the Capability Approach in this instance, where pain was Nicholas' injustice to be removed, who could have predicted the fallout of more pain and injustice, especially in the face of so much energy and knowledge? Removal of an injustice that some might argue is part of nature's way had frightening consequences for us.

Now, I no longer hope for a future full of active verbs for Nicholas. I have accepted that he chooses to remain in bed almost all of his days because that is where he is most comfortable. Nicholas' capabilities of being pain free and maintaining his dignity through choice and self-direction merge in his lifestyle nowadays. The German film director Werner Herzog once made a film about people with disabilities whom, he said, "experience the world on a very reduced level, but very richly." The riches that Nicholas enjoys are his friendships with his caregivers and with his friends and family. And belonging through friendship for someone who is homebound is different, but no less possible or vital.

One life lesson that I have learned in parenting Nicholas is that while adversity is a given in everyone's life, the choice of what to do with that adversity can spell the difference between fulfillment and misery. It is not a "Pollyanna" version of coping that I mean to describe, but rather an idea of converting life circumstances into something good. I recoil from those who seek to sell illness or disability as a "blessing" or "gift." Disabling conditions are a fact of life — they just *are*. Nicholas and others like him are powerful ambassadors for how to live well within limits. It requires imagination and determination to live well within limits, qualities Nick has in spades. And the best aspect of Nick's life is time spent with his many loyal, kind and fun friends.

How does Nicholas assess the quality of his own daily life? Amartya Sen describes the phenomena of adaptive preferences: those choices we make in circumstances of deprivation because other choices seem outside the realm of possibility. Nicholas exercises his adaptive preferences by saying that he is no longer interested in events and activities outside of his bedroom. But Nicholas prefers to view this as anything but tragic. There may be an important game on television he doesn't want to miss, or a new computer game to try out. He chooses a series of interesting activities to pursue each day within the small sphere of his room, and he is happy. With each new blog entry, he is proud. With a delivery of personal business cards, he is excited. He is a young man with a busy agenda, good friends and big plans for the future.

CHAPTER THIRTEEN

Learning and Belonging

A sense of belonging is a powerful ingredient of wellbeing. Jim and I have positioned our family in the company of supportive family and friends over the years, but strangers have sometimes been cruel. Once, after a particularly painful procedure at Great Ormond St. Hospital in London, I took Nicholas to McDonald's for a treat. Nicholas was about seven years old and was happy and excited to be having his meal with its plastic prize tucked in the bag between the burger and fries. I was feeding Nick as I chatted away to him, giggling about the nurse who did not understand his gesture of sticking his tongue out when she cooed innocently, "Now, that wasn't so bad was it?" I didn't see the waiter approach our table, but there he was, red-faced, standing beside us. "The elderly couple at the corner table have complained about you being here and feeding your son," he said, obviously embarrassed. I looked over at these white-haired people who were glaring at us, grim-faced, angry and challenging. "They said that you shouldn't be in a public restaurant. I am going to move them to another table. I wanted you to know in case you heard them talking. I am really, really sorry." I looked at Nicholas who was looking particularly adorable that day, dressed in a designer outfit for the hospital visit. I took Nicholas' hand and said in voice loud enough for the couple to hear, "Nick, those poor people have no love in their hearts. Perhaps their mummies didn't love them enough. We need to pray for them immediately because they are very sad." I took Nick's hand in mine and actually bowed my head, saying a short public prayer as Nick laughed at my nerve.

Many times I have been told that Nicholas, as a wheelchair user, represents a health and safety hazard in case of fire. On that basis, he has been barred from entering ice rinks, bowling alleys and restaurants. The times that Nicholas has been refused a place at school are too many to write about. The common refrain though, was "I am sure your son's needs could be much better met at another school; one that has more resources." Throughout Nicholas' educational career, there have been wonderful successes and spectacular failures. Those welcoming schools where teachers and students celebrated Nicholas' talents, finding ways for him to participate in every aspect of school life, lit the pathway to community belonging for our whole family.

In 1992, when Nicholas was three and Natalie was just six months old, we moved from Ottawa to London, England. Jim had accepted the position of political director at the High Commission and we looked forward to our first international adventure with the children. For Nick, I had great hopes for Conductive Education, a therapeutic method of teaching children with movement disorders how to be functionally independent, and I knew that there was an excellent preschool in the city that specialized in these techniques — the Hornsey Centre.

Nicholas' arms and legs were very stiff, especially when he was excited. He had no purposeful movement of any kind. He would arch his head and trunk backwards and could not, for example, sit independently without falling. Having sampled Conductive Education in Ottawa with our therapist Rosalind, I knew that proponents of the system frowned upon the usual assistive devices, such as wheelchairs, preferring to use simple wooden furniture with lots of built-in grab bars. I arrived at the Hornsey Centre with three goals for Nicholas: to sit independently, to play with a toy by himself and to transfer without assistance from a chair to another seat nearby. In his two years at the centre, Nicholas never actually achieved any of these goals, although he did make some progress in the sitting department. He learned to hold a drinking cup and feed himself a sandwich, albeit with lots of messy spills. I loved the idea of Conductive Education because I believed in the power of learning to overcome not only ignorance, but disability. It spoke to the strong determination to do with intellect and willpower that I was sure could be inspired in Nicholas. At that time, I still suffered from the delusion that my will could overcome the powers of nature that drove Nick's limbs to be stiff and dysfunctional. I couldn't accept that no therapy, surgery or equipment could halt the twisting of Nick's spine or the tightening of his muscles.

The Hornsey Centre was boot camp for kids with cerebral palsy. The staff weren't rude, but they were results-oriented and Nicholas looked like a difficult case. The best students were those with athetoid or ataxic cerebral palsy, those for whom balance and uncontrolled movements were more problematic. For them, learning to rely on grab bars to achieve independent mobility and to perform other basic functions of daily life was achievable and constituted a real reason to celebrate a hopeful future. Parents who had just one child and were able to incorporate rigorous practice of the method at home were championed by the school administration. One evening, I decided to attend a parent meeting to view a home movie made by one young mother. The principal introduced the film as a fine example of what all parents should do with their child at home. We all watched her little girl being coaxed by her parents to incorporate her school learning into each part of her day at home. "Say with me Sarah, I lift my left arm up. Up…up…up." In went Sarah's left arm into the shirt sleeve. "Now hold your sock and pull. Hold…hold..hold. Pull…pull…pull." Sarah pulled up her socks. Outside in the park, Sarah was shown peddling her own tricycle, later at home, feeding herself a biscuit. In the bathroom, she brushed her teeth as she sang, "Brush your dirty teeth, brush your dirty teeth, brush your dirty, brush your dirty, brush your dirty teeth!" I always thought "dirty" was an odd adjective for teeth, but eventually I became so used to this tune that the up and down movements associated with the song became second nature to everyone in my family.

As I watched the film, my cheeks began to burn and my chest felt tight. As the film ended, the centre's director stood and thanked the young mother. Then she turned to the rest of us and said, "This is an excellent example of what can be done if one is determined to do the work and implement at home what your children are learning at school. Your children's progress is up to you."

I was furious. I felt threatened, defensive and humiliated. Just the day before, I had dropped in unannounced to peek at Nicholas from the darkened observation room with its one-way mirror. Nicola, the teacher, was trying unsuccessfully to persuade Nicholas to feed himself. His sandwich kept crushing in his palm, then falling to the floor. There was nothing left that could be held or even eaten; it was just a dense, dirty ball of squashed bread. "Nicholas is NOT doing well today." The teacher glared at Nicholas as she made this pronouncement to her colleague, "Not well at all!"

I opened the door and stepped into the classroom. Flustered, Nicola greeted me much too cheerily and made a show of helping Nicholas take a bite of his dessert. I began to think that perhaps Conductive Education was not the panacea to address disability that I thought it was. Andras Peto, a Hungarian innovator, had devised Conductive Education in order to teach children with disabilities in his country how to walk and perform simple, daily tasks unaided. Without these abilities, children in Hungary were excluded from attending school. A method created for reasons of belonging and inclusion was beginning to make me feel very alone. Nicholas wasn't making progress and it felt like my fault.

About this time, another mum at Hornsey told me that her daughter was having speech therapy at a place called the Cheyne Centre. More and more hallway chat seemed focused on a miracle worker called Helen Cockerill who used a technique called Special Time to get non-verbal children talking.

I managed to get an appointment at Cheyne and we arrived at the appointed hour in front of a Victorian brick building that faced the river Thames. Looking up, I groaned at the number of steps leading up to the entrance doors. "It's a listed historical building," the receptionist apologized. "The heritage department won't let us install a ramp." Like every other parent coming to the Cheyne Centre, I carried Nicholas' wheelchair up the stairs, then returned to the car, scooped Nicholas up in my arms and ferried him to the lobby. A young woman in jeans and a blonde ponytail greeted us with a broad smile and a friendly Yorkshire accent. "Hello, chicken," she said to Nicholas, "I'm Helen." She led us downstairs to a basement warren of peeling hallways until we reached a door decorated with picture symbols resembling hieroglyphics. The small room was filled with toys, and Nicholas arched his back and kicked out his legs, as if pumping his knees would make the play come faster. Helen sat cross-legged on the floor with Nicholas looking out from the crook in her legs. I left the wheelchair in the hallway as Helen began speaking directly to Nick. "Your playtime here is called Special Time, Nick. I will help you, but we will play as if I am not really here. You will tell me what you would like to play with and I will help you. I will count you down to start. Ten…nine…eight…" The room silent now, Nicholas began to slowly look around. His eyes lit on a Lego train set. Helen said quietly, "You are looking at the train set, we'll go play with it. The train goes Choo! Choo!" Nicholas smiled. "You're smiling, you want more." As I watched Helen and Nicholas in a bubble of intense listening pleasure, I thought how wonderful, how seductive and how rare it is to have such complete attention of another person. No wonder Nicholas was smiling!

Later, when we got home, I plopped Nick down into the armchair in our family room and flicked on the television while I tidied up the toys and dishes that we had abandoned on the floor earlier that day. "Ahhh," said Nick. "What?" I asked, not bothering to look at him. "Ahhh," he repeated, now looking at the lamp on the table beside him. "What — you want me to turn on the light?"

"Ahhh." I turned on the lamp and returned to scraping some crumbs off the carpet. "Ahhh," said Nicholas again, looking hard at the lamp. "What, you want me to turn OFF the light?"

"Ahhh!" said Nick, giggling now. "Ahhh! Ahhh!" Light on! Light off!

I telephoned Jim at the office and cried, "Nicholas is

talking! He told me to turn the light on and then to turn it off!" I was laughing, I was so happy.

When I think of this experience in the context of the Capability Approach, a couple of personal truths are revealed. When we arrived in London, I had been clear and unequivocal on the central capability of independent physical function for Nicholas. He was a toddler and action is a toddler's modus operandi. The fact that he did not achieve the goals that I set for him offered me an early lesson in humility where parenting is concerned. But it was also a lesson in understanding the Capability Approach. Perhaps independent physical function wasn't so central to a life Nick valued after all. Would Nicholas have experienced a communication breakthrough if he hadn't been to Conductive Education boot camp where self-reliance was the imperative? Probably not.

But our experience of throwing out old truths and finding new pathways for growth was made possible by choices that could be considered mistakes. The fact that the Hornsey Centre staff valued functional goals for Nicholas over and above the integrated goals of "Nick in our family" turned out to be harmful to me as a mother. The wellbeing of children and their parents is so deeply interconnected that usually parents cannot separate the two. Certainly, I couldn't. In the case of children with disabilities, this extreme closeness lasts much, much longer into adulthood. When a mother experiences a quality of love that is desperate and feels hopelessly inadequate at times to meet her child's needs, her sense of wellbeing is very poor. I used to wonder why, in aid poster images of African mothers holding their starving babies, these mothers were never looking at their offspring. When I felt that I was failing Nicholas, I averted my eyes from him too. Systems in place to assist children with disabilities must examine their programs through the lens of family. Parent supports, or lack of them, must take into account their rebound effect on children.

The fact that Hornsey staff measured success by standards other than Nicholas' own personal bests could have been harmful to Nick. But Nick has always been a resilient and positive person. His response to angst-ridden teachers was to fall off his bench laughing, so that he found himself often banished to the hallway, still chuckling. I sized up our situation and saw that Nicholas had learned to be an actor in his own life. He hadn't learned to play with a toy by himself, but he had learned to initiate, to imagine and to be more fully human. After Conductive Education, a report with "smiles a lot" would never be in the cards again. And certainly, the independent spirit combined with the early communication skills Nick gained in these early years of life made belonging and social ease much easier for him later on.

After two years at the Hornsey Centre, I decided to put Nicholas back into a regular neighbourhood school setting in London. I knew about a school in nearby Hampstead that had already admitted a young boy with disabilities similar to Nick's. An elevator had been installed in the building, and the boy's mum told me she'd managed to secure a range of supports. I filed an application for Nicholas and proceeded to wait for a reply. A letter finally arrived. I ripped it open, only to find the familiar words: "We are sure that Nicholas' significant needs could be much better met elsewhere." I tried to reason and then plead with the head teacher, but to no avail. I was angry and desperately worried about our future without a plan. I hadn't counted on being turned away. Carol Greenaway, our educational psychologist and kind co-strategist, came with me to visit a couple of special schools on offer. In the parking lot after the visit, we looked at each other over the car roof and shook our heads simultaneously. When we were informed by the teachers that parents were not welcome to make unannounced visits to their children at school, we knew these places were out of the question for Nicholas. "God knows what they get away with!" Carol exclaimed and I couldn't have agreed more.

By now, Nicholas was five years old. It was late June, and we still didn't have a school place organized for September. One day, in desperation, I telephoned Robinsfield School, the elementary state school at the end of our street. I knew Robinsfield wasn't wheelchair accessible in the least, but I was grasping at straws. I remember describing Nick's needs to Sheila Sansbury, the head teacher, then sighing, "I suppose there's no way you would want my son."

"WANT him, He's in!" she practically shouted. "Our school *needs* your son."

"But your school isn't even wheelchair accessible," I spluttered.

"Architecture, dear!" she sang. "It's only architecture!"

June Simson, the special education director for our area of London at the time, was sceptical at first about the workability of having Nick at Robinsfield, but she decided to allow the experiment of his placement to go forward. A "good" bureaucrat, June would eventually become a powerful asset in accessing the supports Nick needed and dreaming up workaround solutions for even the most intractable problems.

A caterpillar, battery-powered stair climber was purchased to bring Nicholas from classroom to cafeteria and playground. Two support workers were hired to job-share in assisting Nicholas with all aspects of his school life. A part-time specialist teacher was identified to help Nick learn his reading and talking computer skills. With help, Nicholas learned alongside his peers. He learned to understand the natural world and to imagine experiences outside his own. Robinsfield was the best little school in the world and he was its star pupil.

In 1996, we moved back to Ottawa. I knew that I wanted to replicate Nicholas' Robinsfield experience in Canada, so I arrived home armed with a video showing snippets of Nicholas learning and playing in his neighbourhood school alongside his able-bodied London peers. A date was set in late August for the IPRC (Independent Program Review Committee). This group would decide where Nicholas would be placed in school and what kind of supports he would have. I knew that Nick's needs would be considered, but so would shrinking budgets. I had prearranged for a video monitor and had prepared handouts for the committee, which included photos and testimonies of Nick's mainstream success story. It felt like a parole hearing and the prisoner was me. I decided to exude confidence, middle-class entitlement and prayed that Nicholas himself, along with the English accents of his mates would work a charm offensive. It worked — he was assigned the school of my choice, Churchill Alternative Public School. The alternative schools in Ontario are modelled after the British Infant School system, so Nicholas would have the same active, experiential learning as at Robinsfield. There would be plenty of opportunity for chatter and experiments, with room for his wheelchair at tables of organized chaos. I was triumphant and hopeful for the next phase of Nicholas' school life.

At Churchill, Nicholas was blessed by terrific teachers, a wonderful nurse and an educational assistant who became expert in the technology that allowed Nick to speak using his special computer. During grade five medieval studies, Nicholas played the part of a feast guest, speaking his lines on cue through the computer: "Mmmm, this is good pheasant!"

It was no wonder that after four years at Churchill, a change to middle school seemed akin to free-diving. Adding to our anxiety was the fact that Terry, Nick's educational assistant, announced plans of a move to Toronto in order to pursue disability studies. We chose to continue Nicholas in the alternative system. However, Summit Alternative School was not a roaring success. Despite best efforts by the educational assistant there, teachers were bemused by Nick's presence in class. Primary-school chums who used to welcome him onto pickup hockey teams at recess, now ignored Nick's presence in the hallways. Girls checked their makeup, boys checked their iPods. Nicholas' hip was a problem and surgery, I knew, was imminent. After one year, I decided to move Nicholas to a special school for grade eight. Indeed, Nicholas spent most of his eighth grade in hospital because of surgery and other medical problems. Probably, that was a good thing, given the level of academic rigour. For Nicholas, learning wasn't a feature of the school year in 2001.

The following year, there was one option for Nicholas in the special school setting. The Ottawa Technical Learning Centre purported to offer students with physical disabilities a safe haven for studying the provincial curriculum. It turned out to be neither safe, nor studious. "The Unit" for teens with physical disabilities was located upstairs, separated from the vocational high school on the main floor. When I suggested that Nicholas should attend a class in English literature, the director responded that I find a community volunteer to accompany him downstairs for the duration of the class. No staff members were available for such excursions. Neither was anyone available to change Nicholas when he had an unscheduled bowel movement. He would have to wait until "changing time," due to staff shortage. The final straw was when a sympathetic teacher reported that Nicholas was part of class that studied "beading." Students were taught how to string beads to make jewellery. Nicholas has neither hand function nor vision.

He stared at the ceiling throughout that class and thought (probably) about Harry Potter. I taught Nicholas to be polite and he didn't complain, but I did. He was out of there the following year.

Not only was Nicholas' new high school on the other side of our city, but the exclusion he suffered within the school walls was the source of great loneliness in our family. In grade nine, Nicholas spent a long time in hospital, but no one from school except for his adult helpers came to visit. Other parents weren't neighbours, so no one brought food to our door. It was a lonely time.

We lived directly across the street from a Catholic high school. I had spoken to the principal on several occasions and he was amenable to the idea of having Nicholas attend, but he was wary and made no guarantees. "We would do our best," was his guarded refrain. Finally, the bitter experience of the previous year forced me to swallow my fear and say, "We would like to come to Notre Dame." Once again, the best solution to learning and belonging turned out to be on our own street. The Catholic ethic meant that students were assigned to be buddies to Nick during lunch hour. Nicholas was encouraged to become the sports reporter for the school paper. He was active in each of his classes and struggled to complete his homework on time. At the end of his final year, Nicholas was nominated for a "Spirit of the Capital Youth Award." Cathie Healy, special teacher and special friend, prepared his nomination letter. She wrote:

It is an immense pleasure to recommend Mr. Nicholas Wright for a Spirit of the Capital Youth Award in the area of Academic Perseverance.

Nicholas is an exceptional young man who came to Notre Dame High School two years ago. His presence has enriched the community of Notre Dame. Each day he extends to all a genuine love of life that reminds us to appreciate all that we have and to take advantage of the opportunities that are presented to us. Nicholas has an unwavering ambition to succeed to the best of his abilities and this dedication to fulfill his potential is an ongoing source of inspiration to all who have the privilege of knowing him.

Nicholas has multiple disabilities. He was born with cerebral palsy which means that he must face every day with pain that is exhausting and unrelenting. Joint dislocations caused by his bones growing faster than his muscles cause agonizing spastic pains. He has very limited use of his limbs. He also has great difficulty speaking. He can articulate some words and with the use of an amazing technological device, the Dynavox, he can communicate by utilizing a set of head switches. Nicholas also has cortical visual impairment, seizure disorder, abnormal tone difficulties, nutritional difficulties and developmental delays. He has a specialized wheelchair and his own change room where a plinth and a power lift are located. It is important for Nicholas to be moved from his wheelchair to the plinth so that he can stretch out his limbs. He has a full-time educational assistant, Mr. Nash, as well as a registered nurse, Mrs. McDonald, who provide needed assistance each day. His educational team further includes:

speech-language pathologists, occupational therapists, a phys-iotherapist and an itinerant teacher of the visually impaired. Nicholas' difficulties and the assistance needed to meet these difficulties are noted as realities of Nicholas' day each and every day. It may seem that given the extent of Nicholas' challenges that it would be impossible for him to demonstrate academic perseverance. The fact that Nicholas demonstrates formidable academic perseverance on an ongoing basis is the marvel that led to this nomination.

Nicholas' official placement as noted on his Individual Education Plan is "Regular Class with Resource Support and Monitoring" which means that Nicholas is fully integrated into regular classes. He has a timetable and courses in keep-ing with other students his age. He attends classes, participates in discussions, studies, does homework, completes assignments and takes tests. He follows modified programs in his courses and he works extremely diligently to meet the expectations of these modifications. He is an exceptional auditory learner and he has a fantastic memory. Most importantly, he is actively engaged in his learning and keen to gain as much as he can from his classes. In cooking class, Nicholas became the chief food sampler and actively participated in cooking labs. In reli-gion, he painstakingly put together an oral presentation which was loaded onto his Dynavox and delivered in front of his class. It took a great deal of courage for Nicholas to make this pre-sentation as he is naturally shy, but he rose to the occasion and received many accolades. In drama class, Nicholas overcame nervousness to rehearse, don a costume, watch for cues and play a role in a dramatic performance. He loves literature and is a natural in English class. His English teacher indicated that a poetry poster assignment surpassed expectations and was used as a model for others to follow.

Examples of high achievement and academic perseverance could easily be made for Nicholas in all of his classes. It is important to note that Nicholas not only seeks to achieve in his regularly assigned classes, but he is an active participant in extra-curricular activities. He has written sports reviews of Notre Dame's athletic teams for our newsletters and he has made submissions to our yearbook. He is able to access a word processor by using a cable that is attached to his Dynavox. This system allows him to express his views quite well but he must be very patient as the process is very labour-intensive.

Nicholas is a well-rounded young man with many interests. Anyone who meets Nicholas will quickly learn that he is an avid sports fan. His three favourite sports are wrestling, hockey and soccer. He is a great supporter of Notre Dame's sports teams and regularly attends home games. He also enjoys watching intramurals. He is fiercely competitive and fiercely loyal.

The descriptor provided by the "Spirit of the Capital Awards" states that a student who is being considered under the category of academic perseverance must be "excelling in school and expressing genuine interest in both helping others and overcoming odds." Nicholas excels in his classes. On report cards, teachers note his unfailing positive attitude, his great efforts to put forth his best work, his wonderful sense of humour and his willingness to express his opinions honestly and sometimes forcefully. He certainly helps others. Students learn from Nicholas; his solid determination to succeed allows others to realize that there are no excuses not to try one's best. Nicholas motivates others. He has never returned to school with unfinished homework which is a record that many of his peers can only admire. He models best practices at all times as his class work always reflects effort and thought.

In terms of overcoming odds, not enough can be written to adequately express the degree to which Nicholas has overcome and continues to overcome odds. Mr. Nash has worked extremely closely with Nicholas as his Educational Assistant and he expresses awe in the fact that although Nicholas has faced so much adversity in his young life, he radiates good cheer. He meets every daily strain with incredible fortitude and resilience. Unbelievably, his morale never seems to falter and he goes into every class with the brightest of smiles. A person cannot help but feel better when around Nicholas. Mr. Nash observes that Nicholas "is so full of life, everyone who takes time to get to know him can be nothing but enamored with him."

Nicholas' nurse notes that not only does he overcome daily physical handicaps but he also handles the normal personal adjustments experienced by any sixteen-year-old young man. She says that in her view, he is not a patient; he is a teenager who has hopes and dreams and who is working hard to realize them.

Nicholas Wright is the physical embodiment of perseverance and it can be argued that this perseverance stems from personal courage. Nicholas' physical conditions undeniably take a toll on his body and can sap him of energy. Nonetheless, he finds reasons each day to laugh. His school year is not without interruptions. At times he has needed to be hospitalized due to medical complications, but his awesome willpower to fight for health is partially based upon his desire to return to school. If academic perseverance implies a firmness of mind in face of extreme difficulty, then Nicholas has a mind of steel.

Two very close friends are Alex and Sam Allard. Alex is in grade nine and Sam is in grade seven. These brothers have developed a close bond with Nicholas and they spend many lunch hours and after-school hours with him. Alex and Sam describe Nick as their "big buddy" who is funny, easy to get along with and very talented. Alex states that in his opinion Nick has "the courage of a lion and the energy of a monkey." The brothers are hopeful that Nicholas will be chosen for this award because "it would make his day and he would smile and that smile will light up the world."

The educational team of Notre Dame High School can think of no student more deserving of the Academic Perseverance Award than Nicholas Wright. Nicholas finds ways to succeed in school that fosters his education, inspires others and enriches his community. What more can we ask of a student?

Nicholas did win this award and on June 2, 2005, we all attended a formal dinner at the Ottawa Congress Centre where Nicholas was presented with a $1,000 cheque. Nicholas asked his educational assistant to deliver his acceptance speech. This is how Nick accepted his award:

I would like to thank all the members of The Spirit of the Capital Youth Awards committee for this award. This award makes me both happy and proud. I am proud of my school, my teachers and my friends for working together to help me achieve academic success at Notre Dame High School. I am proud of my family: Mom, Dad, Natalie, for their unfailing love and support. I am also proud of myself for always trying my best. I thought that I would share with you my secrets of perseverance. Talking about pain or ongoing challenge is very boring to me. I would choose having fun and learning at school over sitting home and complaining any day. I will never give up in school because, frankly, I am just too curious and excited to find out what is going to happen next in each of my classes. Some people call this approach having a positive attitude; I call it wanting to express my opinions. I have opinions in my personal life, my school, my community, and my country. And if I want people to hear my opinions, I know I have to be involved. I know how to find information about my interests, and how to use that information. I AM NEVER BORED!!! My advice to other students is to keep trying, even if it takes a long time to achieve academically. The world is far more interesting if you know something about it. At times we all may face some difficulties, but it is important to remember to never give up, and never give in. Thank you all, and good luck.

For good measure, Nicholas insisted on including the lyrics to the theme song of the Liverpool Football Club in place of a bio in the awards program.

You'll Never Walk Alone

When you walk through a storm

Hold your head up high

And don't be afraid of the dark

At the end of the storm

is a golden sky

And the sweet silver song of the lark.

Walk on, through the wind,

Walk on, through the rain,

Though your dreams be tossed and blown.

Walk on, walk on, with hope in your heart

And you'll never walk alone!

You'll never walk alone.[26]

For children and families, the school is the centre of belonging. Our daughter Natalie's sense of community belonging was rooted in her schools as well. Every parent will look at the range of options open to them and choose a school that best suits the character of their child, balanced with the needs and values of family. The same is true for children with disabilities, but those times that Nicholas has been in a special school — especially one far from home, were times when we all felt isolated and lonely. There were no parent volunteer nights, no Halloween parties, no garage sales to raise extra funds, no "bring your pet to school day" and certainly none of Nick's school friends dropping by to play. Our local community centre did fill the gap partially, with its family swim times and accessible playground. However, the feeling of being "normal" in your neighbourhood is often very difficult to achieve for families like mine. But Nicholas' nomination letter for a Spirit of the Capital Youth Award is a powerful testament to the belonging that Nicholas achieved for himself at his high school. And that sense of being known and loved spilled over to our whole family. Teenaged checkout clerks at the local grocery store would stop and ask if I was Nick's mum. "Nick's in my history class…tell him I said Hi!" they would cheerily say as they handed over my purchases.

Nowadays, Nicholas no longer goes to school, but he studies nevertheless. He has taken three courses over the Open University in London, an online higher learning institution in the UK. Most recently, he completed a course titled "Computing for Business and Pleasure." Nicholas is learning to be a seller on eBay and now has the skills and knowledge to direct the growth of his small business. These days, Nick spends most of his time lying down in bed due to chronic pain in his back and hip. There, he is comfortable and has discovered a new belonging in the alternative reality of virtual worlds. His newest gaming device allows him to create a character who is able-bodied. Nick's caregiver takes direction on how the "virtual Nicholas" should dress, where he should go and what he should say to others in this parallel universe.

At first, Nick did not bother to put shoes on his character's feet. But after an hour of exploring the virtual city square when another female character asked him about his barefoot status, he decided to give his virtual self a pair of shoes. This is Nick's first opportunity to observe himself interacting with others. He is learning to navigate social relationships without the burden of such a visible disability skewing others' perceptions of his personhood. We have only begun to explore the possibilities of virtual worlds, but under the collective *protective* eye of Nick's carers and family, he very well may find another sort of belonging.

Yet there is no danger of Nicholas devaluing his real-time friends. For his twenty-first birthday recently, Nick organized a party consisting of a ball hockey game in a corner of Hyde Park in London near our home. Everyone had NHL jerseys, and all of our caregivers came to play. Nicholas tended goal and made many great saves, thanks to the width of his chair. Afterwards, it was home for pizza, beer and presents. Of course, Nicholas' caregivers are paid for working their shifts. But on that day, everyone came because they love my son. Many carers who have moved on have stayed in touch, and some have come back to visit. A few remain lifelong friends. I know that all of Nick's caregivers will say that they are paid in money, but also reap the benefits of a deep and abiding friendship with every member of my family. Now that Nicholas has survived to the ripe old age of twenty-one, we look for belonging in small spaces — Nicholas' bedroom will do fine.

CHAPTER FOURTEEN

Capable Me

Mothering a child with medical needs is a very public but lonely endeavour. Public, because a myriad of professionals weigh in with opinions on how Nicholas should eat, breathe, talk, sit and even be held, but also lonely because all these prescribed therapies are carried out with your child alone at home. There are no neighbourhood mother–toddler groups for young children with severe disabilities. Since Nicholas' birth, there have been times when I felt confident about my mothering because I was rested, healthy and enjoyed support in my nurturing role. There were other times when I felt desperately inadequate in meeting the needs of my family: my own physical and mental health failed and I became overwhelmed, exhausted and hopeless. The capabilities of mothering a special needs child, which I will argue are necessary if families like mine are to survive, are 1) the capability to be a good mother; 2) the capability to be supported in that mothering role by the state (formal support) as well as the community (informal support); and 3) the ability to have a roughly normal trajectory of caring in years, including some hope of a retirement from caring. These three capabilities I believe are matters not just of ethics, but of justice. A fair trajectory of my caring years should not include me changing Nicholas' diapers when he is thirty-five and I am seventy. A just and good society should involve a public/private partnership to support its most vulnerable citizens. It is exactly our society's status quo of dysfunctional push-pull between public and private responsibility for people with disabilities that has painted families, especially mothers, into a bleak corner. Using Sen's Capability Approach as a basis for evaluating my own experience, it is clear that an overhaul of the current arrangements among families like mine, communities and governments is required.

To understand the current political and societal attitudes toward those with dependency needs, a little should be said about the postmodern history of how we cared for and thought about people who required the help of others to survive. The 1980s, the decade of Nicholas' birth, was a time of enormous economic growth. We all felt the rush of individualism, optimism and power. I traded my high heels for running shoes for the walk to work; I did high-impact aerobics on cement floors. We planned our days off around shopping for Art Deco antiques and gourmet cooking with friends. When Nicholas was diagnosed with cerebral palsy, we were told by the neurologist to consider placing him in residential care. "I have seen people waste their whole lives caring for a son or daughter with a severe disability at home," the doctor said. Jim and I agreed that any notion of placing our son in care was barbaric and we never returned to that man's offices.

What we hadn't considered was that no such option for placement existed anyway. We were like newlyweds who could not conceive of the need for a prenuptial agreement. We simply could not imagine being unable to cope with or being incapable of meeting Nicholas' needs. We could not comprehend ever being unable to cope happily with any eventuality involving our son. We had love, strength and brains; of course we would prevail!

The movement for inclusion of people with disabilities really got going in the early 1990s. It was the first year of that decade when the assessing team of authorities had given us no choice but to place Nicholas in a preschool for "mentally retarded" children. It was a quiet, caring place, but after a year of being lulled into tolerating having Nicholas outside our home in the company of others, I felt it was time to return to the mainstream. I hadn't bargained for losing all his therapy services in the move. I had found a local preschool that would take him, but the other children with impairments were more able than Nicholas and required much less support. At his old "special school," Nicholas had the services of speech, physical and occupational therapy. In the mainstream, he would receive none of those, and I would instead have to take him on separate occasions to the hospital to receive his treatments. I went from driving Nicholas to and from school once a day to school plus three trips to the hospital every week.

The need to drive Nicholas to so many weekly

appointments made me question how I would meet his nursing needs as well. I knew then that the movement for inclusion shouldn't be at the expense of essential services, and I started the Ottawa Parent Preschool Advocacy Group to push for a fairer deal. This experience of trading inclusion for specialist services proved to be an omen for trends in Canada and the UK. As families like mine chose to care for their children with disabilities at home, residential facilities closed. Special schools closed as parents chose mainstream school settings. Hospitals hopped on the bandwagon by championing "family-centred care," which anyone who has cared for a sick relative knows is a translation for "do it yourself care." Ministries of education co-opted the rhetoric of equality to justify cutting resources for students with special needs. In the early 1990s, I fought along with others for what we believed was a re-imagined future for our children. I remember telling people that Nicholas' classmates at preschool would be his future employers. Nick's class would be part of the first generation of children to grow up with no prejudice against people with visible differences. Our idealistic enthusiasm was fierce, and we strove to reinvent a society that could accommodate our children throughout their lives. The movement for inclusion and disability rights gathered momentum as children with extraordinary needs survived and their numbers grew.

I have always advocated strongly for whatever I thought Nicholas needed at each stage of his life. But I have only recently begun to understand what this advocacy role has provided to me in return. Having a baby whom I could not feed or soothe easily made me feel sometimes like a desperate failure as a mother, but becoming an expert on therapies and political advocacy strategies helped me to experience a sense of strength and control.

Rosalyn Benjamin Darling points out in her research on parents of children with disabilities: "When parents continue to encounter needs that cannot be met by existing societal resources, they may embark on a prolonged career of seekership. The goal of seekership is *normalization*, or the establishment of a lifestyle that approximates that of families with only nondisabled children. Seekership results in advocacy and activism when certain situational contingencies or *turning points* occur."[27] Such activism Darling calls "entrepreneurship." One has to be socialized into the role of entrepreneur, and socialized I was. The confluence of the changing role of women, opportunities for our higher education and the booming economy all provided fertile ground for the flourishing of my skills as an entrepreneurial activist. Darling continues: "For most parents, active entrepreneurship ends after they reach what they consider to be normalization," while for some it continues to "crusadership." These are the parents who continue to work for disabled children and adults even when the needs of their own children are met.[28]

Darling is right, at least as far as I am concerned, that activism offered me a sense of power, control and usefulness. Activism was and continues to be a core part of my sense of being a good mother. The opportunity to pursue entrepreneurship in the form of activism did afford me a sense of normalization and provided me with a sense of being a good mother to my son. It still does.

Fostering a sense of community for parents of children with disabilities was possible before technology made that job easier. Thirty years ago, the Easter Seals Society of Ontario built programs of support that were rooted in the wisdom of generations of mothers. A specially trained nurse would befriend a new mother of a child with disabilities and in the course of regular home visits, offer all sorts of practical advice and assistance. Mothers and some fathers were invited to join the Parent Delegate program, offering space for activism and information-sharing. Sadly, both of these programs have been cut and Easter Seals now concentrates on funding special equipment and summer camp experiences. But the opportunity to access disability-related professional support at home, together with the chance to befriend other adults who shared our parenting experience, was a powerful combination of support in the just cause of helping me to be a good mother. Mumsnet and other social networking sites are all right, but nothing can replace face-to-face contact with those who share a very unordinary kind of parenting experience.

CHAPTER FIFTEEN

Dependency Matters

Years ago, I remember driving by a billboard advertising for a charity to help victims of famine in an African country. There was a photograph of a mother holding her emaciated baby. The mother was looking at the horizon, not at her baby. "Hmm," I thought. "Why isn't she looking at her baby?" Then, it dawned on me. How many times had I averted my eyes from Nicholas when I could not feed him or soothe him or ease his pain? One moment, I had judged this mother across the world. The next minute, I felt recognition and shame.

Why should any elected official care what goes on in the privacy of my home? What is the advantage of the state in ensuring that I am a good mother? The vulnerable in communities and those who care for them represent dependency, and dependency is a concept rarely welcome to those fed an ideological diet of independence and self-sufficiency. Dependency is not a dinner-table topic of conversation for those not affected by it personally. But the looming demographics of an aging population place these concerns squarely in hard, economic reality. Failure by elected officials to provide preventative crisis strategies and wellbeing measures for families supporting aged, ailing or disabled loved ones will have dire consequences for both citizenry and government budgets. But government alone cannot possibly allow me to be a good mother to Nicholas by providing him all the care he requires. Innovation in social arrangements and funding for our loved ones with long-term-care needs will be required.

The case of severe disability in the family is worth examining because it is the most extreme of dependency experiences in a community context. Eva Kittay writes: "The birth of a child with very significant impairments may test the limit of the commitment that I take to be the very condition for the possibility of mothering…in my own understanding this felt conviction is so fundamental that it serves as a benchmark. The extent to which a woman cannot realize it (in the idiom appropriate to her own culture) because of adverse social, political or economic conditions, to that extent she faces an injustice. I take it then that the requirement to be able to mother, that is, to realize the condition for the possibility to mother, constitutes one of the "circumstances of justice."[29] Here, Kittay could be referring to the African mother with her baby on the poster, but she could just as easily be referring to mothers like me.

On December 26, 1999, a ten-year-old boy with severe cerebral palsy was brought to the Emergency room of a Delaware hospital and abandoned there by his mother.

What made this story so newsworthy was the identity of his parents: Richard Kelso was a very wealthy local businessman and his wife, Dawn, was a known advocate for handicapped children. Mrs. Kelso wheeled her son Steven into the ER along with a bag of toys and a note saying the couple could no longer cope. Police were called, and the parents were arrested and put in jail for the night. Mr. Kelso was sixty-two and his wife forty-five at the time of the incident. They had been sleeping in shifts with no nursing assistance over the Christmas holidays.[30] The pure desperation of this couple, their failed efforts at "normalization," and their exhaustion are all miserably palpable in this sad story. The fact that they were arrested and jailed for attempting to relinquish responsibility for their son suggests that the state had coerced this couple into performing twenty-four-hour duties that would be likened to slavery in any other setting. By all accounts, this couple loved their son. But love is sometimes not enough to provide for survival in cases of "do or die" for persons who are entirely dependent. It seems probable that Mrs. Kelso made efforts in the lifetime of her son to be a good mother to him. Her actions on December 26, 1999, suggest that she was defeated by Steven's needs. His needs were so demanding that no one person or even two persons could meet them without an army of helpers. I know something about what she must have felt that night.

On March 15, 2004, Nicholas received his wish from the Sunshine Foundation. He wanted to meet Stone Cold Steve Austin from the World Wrestling Entertainment, and after all he'd been through, I felt he should have anything that made him happy. I have already described Nicholas' experience on this trip, but I kept secret from the children the awful events that followed for Jim and me. Nicholas, Natalie, a young lad to help with lifting and I arrived in New Jersey at our hotel and I immediately laid Nick down in his bed to rest. He was on oral morphine at the time, but the pain was barely controlled. Many nights at home in Ottawa, Nick would wake screaming and I would rifle through the medicine cupboard looking for something I hadn't already given for the pain. If extra Tylenol or Ibuprofen didn't help, I would call the hospital. The anaesthesiologist on call is the physician responsible for narcotic medicines, so I would have the doctor in that position paged. I would hold the phone up to listen to Nick's screams, explain what I'd already given and ask what more I could safely dispense. Too much morphine can stop a person breathing, so getting the correct dosage was crucial. The problem was, I often gave the maximum allowable amount and my boy was still in desperate straits. The on-call doctors were not always helpful. Some anaesthetists do not "do" pain, only operating-room anaesthesia. Some would quickly give up trying to understand Nick's complex history and just tell me to bring him to Emergency — something I could not do several times a week. Twice, the on-call physicians hung up on me.

I was worried about how I would manage Nick's pain in New Jersey. I knew he would be terribly excited meeting his hero and that excitement was a dangerous trigger for pain. But I also knew that Nicholas said making the trip was the best thing that had EVER happened to him. I had packed every bit of pain medicine from the cupboard at home and I intended to use whatever was necessary to keep Nicholas comfortable during the twenty-four hours we were travelling. During the day, I gave him his regular doses of morphine and after the show and meeting with "Mr. Stone Cold," I gave him an extra half-dose of morphine. I knew he'd been terribly excited and I was afraid of the spasm that I was sure would ensue in the night. I lay awake beside him most of the night, repositioning him for comfort and watching his breathing carefully. "Breathe, Nicholas. Breathe…" I whispered.

The extra morphine worked and Nicholas made it through the night and onto the plane the next day. We were bound for Montreal and a planned admission to the Children's Hospital there to seek solutions to Nick's pain. The first few days of his stay in Montreal were, in the words of his nurse "a hurricane of pain." A constant infusion of morphine was started and oral ketamine (a form of anaesthetic) was added for the nerve pain in Nick's foot. The high levels of medication slowed his digestion and he became nauseated. So much dry heaving caused a bleed in his esophagus, and strong anatacids were added to the mix. I remember standing at the pay telephone in the gloomy hallway, relating the desperate events to our rehabilitation nurse in Ottawa. I described the visit to New Jersey, my worries about taking Nicholas home in such distress, and especially my worry about failing him as a mother. I thought that perhaps he should be placed in a long-term-care hospital. Surely they would know how to manage his pain better than me? Surely they would have shiftworkers who would be less exhausted and desperate than me? Perhaps, I imagined, people who knew me would realize the unthinkable, stark gravity of this request for a hospital placement for Nicholas and funds would be found to keep him at home. I was on my knees, begging for help.

Finally, we boarded an ambulance taking us home to our local children's hospital in Ottawa. I carried the Montreal doctors' notes in my lap, recommending a sleep study to ensure breathing safety in the event of necessary morphine increases. I was happy to be going home and I felt that the pain team in Montreal had witnessed enough of pain at a level "10/10" to make their recommendations irrefutable. I had just got Nicholas settled into his room in the Ottawa hospital when my social worker, together with the rehabilitation nurse, knocked at the door. The look on their faces frightened me.

"What is it?" My social worker looked distraught. The nurse said that a child protection charge had been made against me. There would be an investigation into the allegation that I had overmedicated Nicholas in New Jersey, and that because I had indicated extreme levels of stress and exhaustion, I was possibly trying to harm Nicholas. At the very least, I had given extra morphine without a prescription and potentially put his life in danger. I was incredulous, but at that point, I didn't comprehend the full implications of this turn of events. Then I was told that I could not be alone in the room with Nicholas. Easter weekend was coming up and Nicholas could not come home for a weekend pass. I was being investigated as a mother with intent to harm, if not kill, her child. A sense of dread, fear and helplessness oozed its way into my thoughts and dreams. I worried constantly that they might take not only Nick, but also Natalie away from us. It was ironic, I thought, that my greatest fear had been Nick dying.

Trying to reinvent my life without being his mother was an unfathomable task. I had been doing his care for so long, and I defined my own personal worth through advocating for him to have the best of everything. I could not believe that anyone who knew me even a little would think I could ever harm anyone, especially my treasured boy.

At that time, I was already in my second appeal process to the Ontario Ministry of Community and Social Services/Youth Services for more help at home. We had long ago maxed out available resources under the eligibility policy guidelines, and Lynne, our social worker, was helping me to navigate the appeal process. Several rounds of the appeal had resulted in the committee responding that they agreed that our needs outweighed available resources, but there was nothing more they could offer.

For the committee, I had prepared a list of Nicholas' daily care requirements:

- a total of nine medications dispensed via gastrostomy tube 10 times per day, plus pain medication as needed;

- skin-care monitoring and intervention required for tube site in abdomen and pressure sores on elbow and hip;
- repositioning in wheelchair every half-hour for pain and discomfort;
- lifting out of chair into bed 6 times per day for pain;
- changing diapers and skin-care check 6 times per day;
- tube feeding 2 to 3 times per day, each given by pump over a three-hour period, plus 70 millilitres of water given via syringe into the tube 10 times per day;
- venting (allowing air to escape from stomach) from tube 4 times per day; overnight, 8 times repositioning for pain and/or sleep apnea, plus pain medication dispensing on as needed basis;
- recording and reporting pain symptoms for physicians;
- face/hands wash 3 times per day;
- brush teeth 3 times per day, more if not able to take any food or drink by mouth at all;
- shower once per day;
- total clothing change 3 times per day;
- total assistance for eating of oral snacks, monitoring choking;
- careful manicure/pedicure care due to self-injury risk;
- massage and manual traction of limbs for pain relief as needed;
- wiping of nose and of chin for drooling 24/7;
- communication (see Appendix B for how Nick communicates): interpreting each effort to communicate verbally, oral presentation of all new information (due to low vision) such as reading newspaper, books, homework;

- social/emotional: changing television/radio stations, DVD, controlling computer and PlayStation while interpreting events on account of low vision, facilitating friendships and communication with friends/helpers.

Associated risks of not performing the preceding tasks:

- overdose or insufficient dose of medications will result in seizures, diarrhea leading to dehydration or constipation leading to symptoms of bowel obstruction and dehydration due to intolerance of feeds, pain, respiratory failure, death;
- failure to carefully monitor and treat skin breakdown will result in infection, at tube site in abdomen; topical infection will contaminate spinal cord pain pump (located adjacent and requiring injectable refills), causing meningitis;
- failure to reposition in chair and into bed for pain will lead to increased spasm, uncontrolled pain and skin breakdown;
- failure to change diapers will lead to skin breakdown and infection;
- underfeeding via tube will lead to weight loss and dehydration; overfeeding will lead to retching and aspiration pneumonia;
- failure to carefully clean syringes and all tube-feeding equipment may result in gastrobacterial infection;
- failure to vent or decompress stomach via tube will lead to retching, aspiration pneumonia and intolerance of feeds;

- failure to monitor overnight pain and apnea will result in uncontrolled pain and death;
- failure to record and report symptoms of pain will result in escalating symptoms due to lack of treatment;
- failure to maintain proper personal hygiene will result in infection and social isolation;
- improper monitoring of oral feeding will result in aspiration pneumonia and death;
- failure to provide physiotherapy will result in increased pain;
- failure to monitor and manage secretions will result in social isolation and aspiration in the case of flu/cold;
- failure to offer total assistance in psychosocial activities will lead to isolation, boredom and depression;
- failure to facilitate communication will lead to behaviour problems.

The caseworker at the Children's Aid Society and the child protection officer at the Children's Hospital finally completed their investigation of me as a mother.

On June 14, 2004, I received the following letter from our caseworker at Children's Aid.

Dear Mrs. Thomson,
This letter is to inform you that your file with the Children's Aid Society of Ottawa is now closed. The Society became involved with your family following a report that you had given Nicholas too much medication, without seeking proper approval from a medical doctor. Additionally, there was a

concern that you were not effectively managing the stress of Nicholas' care and special needs. After meeting with you and your family, and speaking with many of the community professionals involved with your family, to discuss the concerns, the Society does not feel it necessary to remain involved with your family. The allegations were not substantiated.

To the appeal committee, they wrote:

Dear Mrs. Thomson,
As per our discussions throughout your involvement with the Children's Aid Society of Ottawa, this letter is in support of your family requiring a higher level of community and in-house medical supports to effectively manage Nicholas' ever-changing medical needs.

It is the position of the Society that it is in Nicholas' best interests to return home with his family. It is evident that Nicholas is an integral part of the Thomson/Wright family, with all reports describing a close, affectionate bond between himself, you, his father, and his sister. However, Nicholas' special needs and fragile health place both him and your family in a highly vulnerable position should his needs not be met within his home.

The child protection worker assigned to our case, the author of the two letters, became our advocate with the provincial appeal board. Children in Ontario whose needs exceed the maximum offer of help from the province can appeal to the Office of Child and Family

Advocacy, essentially an ombudsman service with its own appeal board called IMPAC. That committee had already garnered plenty of practice working with families such as mine. One mother, Anne Larcade, had tried to launch a class action suit against the province for forcing her (and other parents) to give up custody of their children with disabilities when they chose to have them placed in a publicly funded long-term-care facility. Faced with inadequate service provision at home, Larcade and others were told the only way to access more help was to "buy" a residential placement by paying for it with their parental rights. The class action suit failed, but the story made the news.

In 2005, the then Ontario ombudsman, André Marin, issued a scathing report titled "Between a Rock and Hard Place" describing in depressing detail the cases of 113 families who had been forced to relinquish custody of their children with severe disabilities in order to secure round-the-clock services for them; 196 other families were on a waitlist for the same deal with the province.[31] Mothers had to sign away their parental rights and admit to being incapable of caring for their offspring in order to secure services necessary for their child's survival. The either/or of state versus family-care arrangements, with very little in between, is still the status quo in Ontario, but it wasn't always so.

In the early 1980s, the provincial government instituted "Special Needs Agreements" under which families could share care of their disabled child with the Children's Aid Society without giving up custody. In 1997, the government discontinued entering into these agreements, and families were left with no choice but to continue looking after a child whose needs they could not meet or else manufacture child protection issues resulting in the loss of parental custody in order to "buy" care.

On February 7, 2009, the *Ottawa Citizen* printed a story about an Ottawa family who were on the verge of making that painful decision. Penelope McKeague was stillborn, but resuscitated after fourteen minutes, leaving her with multiple disabilities. Shelley Page reported: "Penelope had screamed for hours, screamed like she was possessed, screamed past exhaustion. Nothing would bring her comfort. Not even a steaming hot bath to loosen her tightening, always tightening muscles. Everything makes her frantic. The feel of her clothing. A sudden noise. Her mother's love. 'She doesn't like to be cuddled,' Kristine Gavrel says wistfully."[32] Gavrel, like me, reported wanting to be a mother, not a nurse. She felt a failure as a mother and incapable of soothing an inconsolable baby daughter who could not tolerate any form of stimulation, including being held. "She already had the worst birth imaginable. She was stillborn. And now to get proper care we have to give her away?" asks Ms. Gavrel. "That's like another death. This is just a horrific situation. There is a huge stigma to saying you can't care for your child. I am a decent person and a good mother, but in the eyes of society, I won't be."[33]

Under what circumstances can mothers like Kristine Gavrel or me be allowed to mother our children with disabilities? If those disabilities result in needs that are too great for one person to safely provide care, then what options should exist? The current paradigm of state control or family control with minimal support is clearly failing the neediest citizens. The one reason that Kristine Gavrel and I got into so much trouble with authorities is clear. In our cases, representatives of state-funded institutions applied policy directives without a public acknowledgement that those policies did not serve our families fairly. Policies on child protection or social assistance were never written with our families in mind. Most people, policy-makers included, are not aware that we exist. But people with the highest care needs are surviving, and these are individuals whose care cannot be supported by any one funding entity alone. Separate policy routes such as through the Office of the Advocate for the Child (Ontario) should be much more accessible to families whose needs far exceed the norm. A public–private partnership with shared fiscal responsibilities is the model I believe will be necessary to care for our vulnerable loved ones. Currently, upper limits of home help available from provincial health and social services are too low for children with severe and multiple disabilities. Placement options do not exist except for children who are wards of the state. The public–private sharing of care and costs is a concept that does not appeal to a risk-averse state authority. Leaving aside the ethics of resuscitating a baby after fourteen minutes, should families and governments enter into shared care agreements? We already do so for many seniors. The sons and daughters of parents with dementia who enter care homes do not relinquish their caring relationships with their loved ones in order to secure a placement.

In the future, groups representing seniors could be pitted against those championing people with disabilities, in a fierce competition for public funding earmarked for social care. Substitute decision-making, powers of attorney and other such agreements already exist to assign roles and responsibilities vis-à-vis choosing care options and medical decision-making. Families enter into financial agreements with government-subsidized nursing homes using pension and retirement-fund savings to cover costs. Sons, daughters and other family members continue to play an active role in the life of their vulnerable relative and often contribute towards extraordinary costs in a collaborative manner with extended family. No one would ever expect to give up their family roles and responsibilities in order to gain placement for an aging and ailing parent. And no son or daughter would be expected to give up their employment, savings or home to pay for a parent's care.

So, why do we expect this of young mothers and fathers of children with severe disabilities? Being a good mother means something different to everyone — for me it has always meant help from government in the form of access to long-term-care budgets for high levels of nursing care to keep Nicholas at home. But I know that there will come a time when he has to move into his own "place," and that time is coming soon.

When Nicholas is feeling well, and he often is, his disabilities seem invisible to me. Even though he is nonverbal, he has many meaningful sounds that only those closest to him understand, and we have long conversations on a wide range of topics. His language comprehension is almost perfect, although he has conceptual difficulties in some more abstract forms of reasoning. He has a wicked sense of humour and often has his helpers in helpless fits of laughter. So, although I am sometimes using cases of children who are more globally delayed than Nicholas here, I do that with the intention of underlining the ethics upon which our collective response to extreme dependency rests. It is worth picking apart the worst case scenarios of families like mine because these dramas force us to reckon with the moral fundamentals essential to inventing a social framework that will sustain us through good times and bad. One of the moral underpinnings that I require is the freedom to grow old without being my son's caregiver 24/7. A retirement of sorts, a hope of not changing my son's diapers when he is forty-five and I am past eighty is a moral "right" in my view. Neither is it acceptable for a young child to care for a disabled parent. The natural trajectory of giving care to another is a model for normal here, and our society should use it as a benchmark in policy-making.

In the current dialectic on social inclusion, there is a lot of talk on the subject of reciprocity. "What goes around, comes around" is a phrase often heard. Notions of reciprocity in action have galvanized communities to trade services, such as delivering meals or retired people and taxi drivers befriending shut-ins by shuttling them to medical appointments. But reciprocity is also an ethical idea that underpins our caring for an elderly parent who gave us life and a decent upbringing.

In our family's case, is there any duty of reciprocity here and if so, to whom or what should I (as Nick's primary caregiver) be looking for something in the way of payback for my son's care? Who will repay me for the care I give to my son? Who will care for me and Jim when we are infirm? Obviously, it won't be Nicholas. And Nick will most likely never be employed, so his life exists outside a social contract with the state. He will not pay taxes or contribute to a national pension plan. The case of children like Nicholas who are net consumers of social funds and who will never repay the state by becoming employed is one that poses the most basic of ethical dilemmas. In the context of shrinking national economies, hard questions have to be asked about the human worth of people who will never be employable. Sarah Palin's infamous Facebook post suggesting that "Democrat death panels" might order the euthanasia of noncontributing, dependent citizens, played directly into the worst fears of an aging population. Of course this was transparent, politically motivated fear mongering, but it received some traction because people do fear the natural endgame of the current thinking on dependency. Policies, programs and services are all directed at achieving independence and self-reliance.

But a hardline interpretation of those ethics leads people like Robert Latimer to be isolated in their attempt to bring up a totally dependent child without the help of friends, community or government resources. Such a stance does no favours for the state either, because the risk of catastrophic family breakdown is so high.

So, how might our society begin to think about a fairer deal for supporting vulnerable citizens? Eva Feder Kittay coined the word *doulia* to describe a new paradigm for reciprocity for caregivers in the community. She describes doulia as an ethical principle that recognizes giving care as an important contribution to the overall good of society. "We can ask whether parents or kin who assume the role of caregiver should have claims on the larger society to support them in their efforts to provide care. If, for all the effort and care in raising a child with disabilities into adulthood, there is no payback (conventionally understood) to the society at large, can we still insist that there be a state interest in helping families with the additional burdens of caring for a developmentally disabled child? Is there a state interest in assuring families that their vulnerable child will be well cared for when the family is no longer able or willing to do so?"[34] Kittay answers her own question with a resounding yes and that response is rooted firmly in her own mothering experience. She describes a concept of interdependency or "nested dependencies" that recognizes the inevitability of dependency as a fact of being human. It is via the idea of doulia that reciprocity can be realized through policy because the driving force is an equality that "our full functioning presumes our need for and ability to participate in relationships of dependency without sacrificing the needs of dependents or dependency workers."[35]

Carers' organizations in the UK are acutely aware of how their constituents are often exploited. When the UK government produced a policy on disability titled "Putting People First,"[36] the Princess Royal Trust for Carers published a response entitled "Putting People First—Without Putting Carers Second."[37] For someone like me whose charge is incapable of reciprocating care, this idea is a welcome lifeline. Here Kittay is advocating an ethical framework for governments to look after caregivers so that caregivers can carry out that care without sacrificing their own wellbeing. We know doulia as friends and family members who help a new mother by watching the older children and performing household chores so that the mother can give total care to her newborn. Implicit in this natural family tradition is the understanding that the mother is "owed" care because she is giving care to a much loved, highly vulnerable newborn. Her first priority is to give the best care possible to her beloved charge. But Nicholas is twenty-one years old, and his physical needs are still similar to those of a newborn. What forms of payment can I expect for my years of giving care? Should I have any claim to rest and retirement? And if so, who should provide it to me?

The feminist scholar Arlene Kaplan Daniels coined the phrase *invisible work* to describe the many tasks that women perform in their families and communities. Picking apart our folk understanding of what constitutes "work," Daniels wrote (in 1987):

> We distinguish work from leisure activity (that we *want* to do because we enjoy it) and from other activities in the private realm of life — personal grooming, child care, homemaking.
>
> In modern, industrialized societies, perhaps the most common understanding of the essential characteristic of work is that it is something for which we get paid. This idea is associated with activity in the public world, which is dominated by men and separated from those private worlds of family and personal relationships where women predominate. There may be exchanges in households and friendships, but they are not monetary. Even activity in the public sphere, such as volunteering and community service, is not work if it isn't paid. Any activity we do for pay, wherever it is found, even if we enjoy it, must, by definition, be work.
>
> But any effort we make, even if it is arduous, skilled and recognized as useful — perhaps essential — is still not recognized as work if it is not paid.[38]

Daniels talks about housewives in a slightly less-than-contemporary North American context. But her observations still ring true, especially about contemporary women who assume a full-time caring role. The work of caring has no monetary value, and therefore no moral force or dignity in the public consciousness. Governments have always capitalized on this conception of care that is not "work" to protect their shrinking social care budgets. Market prices affect our definitions of what is work and what is not. Twenty years ago, giving someone a bottle of formula via a stomach tube was a nursing task — today anyone in a family can perform this job, no university degree required and no pay received.

However, consider what is required to bring an elderly relative with dementia to the shopping mall. Can it be called work? Of course it can, but it doesn't have to be paid to be recognized as valuable. There are other kinds of work involved in giving good care.[39] There are qualities that describe a kind person, a good mother, or a good friend, but these same qualities are also central to good care for vulnerable people. Maintaining this height of alertness and level of emotional giving is tiring. A different definition of work is called for if parents like me are to be protected from exploitation, be rewarded for our contributions, and have a hope of retirement from our duties.

The physical and emotional toil of dependency work has something to do with love, but it should never be taken as an extension of it. The extent to which a carer has to become "transparent" in order to provide good care, acutely listening and watching for signs of need or distress, cannot and should not be sustained without reward and rest. Assuming that a more appropriate definition of invisible work will evolve based on the sheer numbers of citizens involved in giving care, what kinds of rewards can society offer? Every individual is likely to seek a personal answer to that question. Certainly, some will want cash compensation either in the form of pension benefits or direct payment. For others, the rewards of familial affection will be satisfactory recompense. But the public knowledge that persons who give care must be allowed to choose *a* reward is the idea I wish to put forward. A person coerced into giving care without regard for their own health, fitness, aspirations or talents is a recipe for bad care with dangerous implications for all concerned.

But, rewards given by the state in the form of payments are hardly ever without strings attached. Funds must be spent on this, but not that. Every expense must be fully accountable on a "worthy" expenditure. A family who receives government assistance to buy food might find itself in hot water if they choose to purchase a Christmas tree instead of a turkey during the holidays.

I am sure that in the case of putting money and power into the hands of individual families, many tax-paying citizens would wring their collective hands at the thought of letting mothers run amok in malls with government funds. My response would be that there will always be a few people who behave badly in the public and private domains. But in a democracy, we do not construct a single public policy based on the poor judgement of a few misguided Canadians. Most parents do their best to nurture their children. It's just that in some cases, it takes a village.

Eva Feder Kittay envisions a new ethic for long-term care by nudging us towards a new conception of equality. She writes: "By viewing our relations to others as nested dependencies, we start to frame equality in terms of our interconnections...for the disabled and their caregivers alike. Each gets to be seen as some mother's child."[40] To position interconnectedness as central to or synonymous with equality is the very core ethic critical to ensuring capability achievement for me and every other member of my family. We are all some mother's child.

CHAPTER SIXTEEN

Being Well

How could anyone possibly measure the extent to which someone has a life that they value and have reason to value? The Capability Approach is a wonderful idea, but it is notoriously difficult to pin down and quantify. Many have tried. Martha Nussbaum wrote her list of ten capabilities. The UN's Human Development Index is an attempt to give form and substance to the approach as a policy tool. And those who study the area of well-being in populations have made significant inroads in quantifying the messy business of individual freedom, potential and happiness.

My foray into wellbeing and assessment happened quite by accident. During my lunch meeting with Professor Sen, he happened to ask me if I was acquainted with Sabina Alkire, a professor of economics at Oxford. I replied that I was aware of her work on human security and economics, but that we had never met. Sen picked up his phone, dialled Sabina, explained my project and passed the phone to me. She was warm and gracious on the call and offered any help and advice that I wanted. Later at home, I emailed to invite her to tea in London and she accepted a few weeks later. As I began to query her work, Sabina mentioned that she had been deeply involved in creating the National Happiness Index for Bhutan. Excited, I blurted, "Do you think you could create an index for my family?" She quickly agreed and we began to talk about the type of index that would work for us. Sabina already knew something about our family and we decided that a simple index measuring our functioning in daily life, together with a couple of indicators related to emotional and spiritual satisfaction, would be appropriate. It would also be short enough that Nicholas could complete it along with the rest of the family.

After our tea, I invited Sabina upstairs to meet Nicholas and show her the photos I planned to use as book illustrations. With a promise to write with an index, she gave me a hug and looked at her watch. "Oh, I'd better go!" she said. "I have a Bhutanese monk with me and I've left him in Oxford Street shopping. He's never been in the West before!"

"Is he alone?" I gasped, laughing. Sabina nodded and she hurried away to rescue her friend.

Several weeks later, the index arrived. A note from Sabina explained that I must decide on three time periods and ask each member of the family how they rated the domains, using a scale of zero (for extreme dissatisfaction) to five (extreme satisfaction). The domains that Sabina identified were:

- Health — energy and rest
- Health: Pain
- Health: Mobility
- Health — mental
- Family Relationships
- Friendship
- Community Support
- Beauty and Creativity
- Education and Learning
- Meaningful Work
- Play and Fun
- Inner Peace
- Spiritual State
- Harmony with Nature
- Self-direction
- Empowered to Act

As for the three time periods, I chose the years 2004, 2006 and 2009. The markers that I used to highlight 2004 were Nicholas' failed hip surgery, his uncontrolled pain and hospitalization in Montreal. The highlight of 2006 was our move to England and settling into life in the UK. By 2009 we felt truly established in London.[41]

The survey results when our scores were averaged to represent the whole family unit were not surprising: 2004 was a very bad year, 2006 was novel and exciting and 2009 was our year of being quite settled and content (see Appendix A for an analysis of the index).

Much more interesting and surprising were the individual scores. Sabina suggested that I attempt to predict the scores of my husband and children. On the part of Nicholas, I predicted very low scores in all domains for the year 2004 and by and large, I was right. I recalled Natalie suffering a sort of malaise that year, with adolescent friendship problems in addition to the usual sources of adolescent angst. I also knew that she felt keenly the distress of her brother and her own helplessness to alleviate it. Her results mirrored my predictions.

I found Jim's results for 2004 astonishing! During that year, he was entirely engaged by the all-consuming nature of his position as political director of the Department of Foreign Affairs and yet, he reported higher levels of general wellbeing and happiness than in either 2006 or 2009. I could never have predicted that!

Jim's results for the year 2004 revealed fascinating truths about the inner workings and resilience of our family. That year, Jim was entirely immersed in serious matters of state — terrorists were striking on multiple fronts in the Western World and Canada had recently committed to sending troops to Afghanistan. All government files related to weapons of mass destruction, rogue states, G8 summits and international peacekeeping were Jim's files. When I looked at his index scores for the year 2004, I felt a sense of personal pride that I had managed to protect my husband so that he could provide for us. Figuratively speaking, if our family were swimming a marathon and Jim was the only person in the boat alongside, we couldn't have him in the water too. We needed at least *one of us* to be functioning and not drowning. Throughout the most difficult times in our family history, I tried to protect Jim from many of the sordid details. And selfishly, I wanted to keep up the pretense of order and normalcy when he came home from work late at night. He would come through the door, give me a kiss, remove his tie and sit down with me in front of the late night news, his dinner tray balanced on his lap.

The move to the UK in 2006 marked a turning point for all of us. Everyone was much happier. Nicholas reported extreme satisfaction in almost all domains. Interestingly though, he experienced relatively high unhappiness in the area of education and learning, even though he completed an online college course during that year. When queried, he replied that he missed the camaraderie of his school environment. Nick's other low score in the domain of spiritual state reflected his opinion that the domain itself was of little importance to him. Natalie reported a healthy improvement from her scores of 2004, but some shortfall from perfect satisfaction was the result of her struggle to make friends during her first year in a new country. My scores, although much improved since 2004, indicated that my recovery from a period of extreme unhappiness (or crisis) was slower than the children's — not an unusual phenomenon for any mother!

Nick's scores for 2009 came as quite a surprise. My predicted scores for him in most domains were quite high — I thought he was happy. I mistook his high scores in the area of play and fun for a high level of general wellbeing. But his low scores, especially in the areas of friendship, family relationships and meaningful work made me feel sad. I queried him about family relationships and he said that of course he missed all our relatives back in Canada, but he also had a complaint about our immediate family. He expressed a sense of frustration that Jim's interaction hadn't changed much over the past few years. Nicholas said that although he had grown into a mature man, his father still addressed him as a teenager. These results prompted a meeting between father and son where both had the opportunity to elaborate on their feelings about evolving relationships.

In Nicholas' case, some of his high unhappiness scores reflected the real lack of opportunity he experiences due to his disability. This applies to the domains of harmony with nature as well as beauty and creativity. In 2006, Nick was more satisfied in these areas, but when I asked him about that, he reported that everything seemed better in 2006 because moving to England was so much fun and exciting.

As a result of the index, I was able to chat with him at length about some ways in which we might change his lifestyle to make him happier. We talked about how to find at least one activity every day that would involve learning and meaningful work. Nicholas indicated that he enjoyed doing the index because his parents and helpers could now help him pursue more fulfilling activities. Nick's wellbeing remains a work in progress.

The index that we used helped everyone in my family

to better understand how we felt about our life opportunities, choices and actions over time. But should such a tool, or a more elaborate version of it, be used by governments to inform policy-making? The Hon. Roy Romanow and others at the Canadian Institute of Wellbeing believe it should. A Canadian index exists, and efforts are underway to develop a composite index — a single number that moves up or down (like the TSX or the DOW Jones Industrial), offering a snapshot of whether or not the overall quality of life for Canadians is going up or down. According to the institute's website:

> The Canadian Index of Wellbeing (CIW) is a new way of measuring wellbeing that goes beyond narrow economic measures like GDP. It will provide unique insights into the quality of life of Canadians — overall, and in specific areas that matter: our standard of living, our health, the quality of our environment, our education and skill levels, the way we use our time, the vitality of our communities, our participation in the democratic process, and the state of our leisure and culture. In short, the CIW is the only national index that measures wellbeing in Canada across a wide spectrum of domains.
>
> The CIW goes beyond conventional silos and shines a spotlight on the interconnections among these important areas: for example, how changes in income and education are linked to changes in health.

The CIW is a robust information tool, one that policy shapers, decision-makers, media, community organizations and the person on the street will be able to use to get the latest trend information in an easily understandable format.[42]

The Canadian index includes four broad categories of wellbeing for assessment: living standards, healthy populations, community vitality and democratic engagement. For example, the following headline indicators fall within the Community Vitality Domain: belonging to community, participation in group activities, volunteering, number of close relatives, providing assistance to others, experience of discrimination, trust, walking alone after dark, violent crime and poverty crime. The indicators are a perfectly good set of subject areas for determining whether an individual, group or population feel relatively safe in the context of their community relationships. But in my family's case, the case of a life with disability, these indicators do not have the potential to tell the "real story." In 2004, for example, the worst year for me and Nick, our scores in many of these indicators would have been high — belying the misery we actually experienced. The story they do not tell is the lack of freedom that we experienced to do anything we wanted due to the oppression of pain and illness. Because I was trying to manage more or less on my own, there was no shortage of caring on my part. I still managed to volunteer at my children's schools that year. My extended family did their best to be supportive. My score in the caring for others category would have been off the scale. Perhaps what this scale lacks is an indicator that inquires whether one has the capability to do something unplanned for fun. Ever. If Mr. Romanow and others at the Canadian Institute of Wellbeing would like to know how many people are affected negatively by disability (and this includes caregivers), a question about spontaneous outings might be a good place to start. And the informational tools for policy-making that encompass the real concerns of those with care needs should be front and centre when it comes to sourcing innovative solutions to serving the needs of an aging population.

CHAPTER SEVENTEEN

Good Ideas and
Practical Solutions

For the first time in history, people with disabilities will have wealth. But, will governments allow them to contribute to their own care and lifestyle? Cost-sharing between ministries, let alone between public and private sources, is a gigantic headache as far as bureaucrats are concerned.

Take our family, for example. I have thought long and hard about how to arrange a safe, happy future for Nicholas outside of our home. Long-term-care hospitals that are operated by the provincial Ministry of Health and Long-Term Care do not want Nicholas because they cannot staff his overnight one-to-one nursing care for sleep apnea. They understand that Nicholas requires facial stimulation when he stops breathing during sleep, but they simply cannot guarantee that someone will be there to do it. The provincial Ministry of Community and Social Services operates group homes for adults with developmental disabilities, but they do not have the complex-care nursing services that Nick requires. Provincially funded spots in group homes for people with developmental disabilities are oversubscribed with long waiting lists, and they would not be suitable anyway for Nick whose needs are primarily health-related.

A fairly recent phenomenon is the cropping up of private "for profit" group homes that cater to individuals, whatever their needs. The uptake on places in these facilities has primarily been from individuals who can manage to pay the private fees by using resources they accrued through a post-accident insurance payout. I decided that Nicholas would need a place at one of these private group homes. From England, I called one of the private homes, out of interest, and asked if they could provide for Nick's needs. "Sure," the woman replied, "we can provide any service that your son requires. And we can add or take away services according to his changing needs." Costs, of course, are astronomical. But on the whole, I thought if money was no object, it would be perfect. Nicholas would be in a home, not a hospital. We would ensure that he always had friends and family in his life through a PLAN network. He could come to our family home for dinner if he felt up to it, because we would ensure that we lived nearby.

I decided to speak to Nicholas. First, I asked him if he would like to move out of our house and live somewhere on his own. I asked him if he ever dreamed of living in his own place. Nick's eyes were wide and his back was arched — a sure sign of panic, so I reassured him that I was just asking for future reference. He eyes narrowed and he considered the question. "Well," he told me, "I would like to live with my old friend John Bilder, or maybe Adam Forster. That would be great! Can I *do* that?" Both John and Adam are former caregivers and John remains a very close, lifelong friend. "No," I replied. "John works full-time and Adam has a new baby now." We both agreed to think about the future and to chat again later.

I resolved to put together a financial and social plan for Nicholas' future that actually felt good to him and to us. I decided that a private group home, if cost-shared between the two provincial ministries concerned with people like Nicholas (Health and Community and Social Services), combined with our private funds, could be the way forward. The Ministry of Health could pay for Nicholas' overnight nursing care and any other costs deemed strictly medical. The Ministry of Community and Social Services could fund the day nonprofessional health-care workers as well as case management fees. Our family would fund the basic housing costs as well as any other fees involving food, friends and fun. Currently, an arrangement such as I have described could never occur under our bureaucracy that defines itself by its silos of funding and function. But the status quo will be forced to change soon, because I am not the only parent who will want to contribute to a high standard of living for her son with high needs. Furthermore, Nicholas is leading the charge of the first generation of children with disabilities to grow up having personal wealth. And he wants to spend it.

Families like mine are resilient. We are capable of surviving a surprising amount of adversity. But we cannot do this unsupported, with no recognition of our contributions to our communities and our country. A new deal for families should include policies that encourage contribution to care without losing state benefits; as well, it should encourage families to save for the costs of care, knowing that governments will not take back those savings in the form of taxes. These are the key elements of a secure future for our vulnerable citizens. Any policy that purports to help citizens have a good life should be *least restrictive* and *most supportive*. PLAN describes such a good life as being supported by caring family and friends, being encouraged to participate in and contribute to one's community, having one's wishes and choices respected, having financial security, living in a place of one's choosing, and being protected from abuse and exploitation. This definition of a good life, applied to all, even the most vulnerable and disabled, presupposes the equal human worth of each individual citizen. It also assumes that with proper support, most people are capable of resolving their own challenges efficiently.

The past half-century has seen the closure of residential care institutions for people with disabilities and growth in numbers of nursing homes for the aged. Who cares for and who pays for all these dependent individuals is a problem governments have struggled with ethically, financially and politically over the years. Governments' first response has been to devolve responsibility for vulnerable citizens to families, usually women. Liberal values of "free and equal" citizenship, combined with a drive for independence originating in the disability movement, have further marginalized those with cognitive disabilities or mental illness. For them, and for their families, independence is a cruel fiction. Compounding the problem for families is the fact that the first response of governments has been to minimize damage to their budgets by limiting access to community care, usually by increasing thresholds of eligibility. Thirty years ago, tube feeding would have been a nursing need requiring hospitalization. Today, families are expected to roll this task into their day alongside walking the dog and fixing school lunches. What to do with people who are completely dependent and whose families cannot or will not support them is a huge problem for contemporary societies. Equality-based policies have failed people with disabilities and their families — we are not a society of equals.

In the UK, a grand social experiment is underway. The Labour government under Gordon Brown took devolution of social care one giant step further by creating personal budgets for those receiving government-funded care at home. Supporters of this regime decry the old system of take-it-or-leave-it day programs, likening this to "someone taking all your money and spending it on things you don't want or need." The UK government at all levels is hoping that people will creatively make their disability-pension cheque go further by being imaginative and flexible. But there is a worry among some that this policy represents state-sanctioned abandonment of its neediest citizens and a downloading of responsibility for their welfare to those who are least able to shoulder it.

One thing is clear. Governments cannot single-handedly provide the elements of a good life for vulnerable people who require care in the community. But families cannot shoulder the burden of care unassisted either.

So what are the roles of families and governments in supporting society's most vulnerable citizens? What kinds of policies can facilitate true partnership between governments and families who seek to care for someone needing help? One such policy is the groundbreaking Canadian Registered Disability Savings Plan (RDSP). In the late 1990s, Al Etmanski of PLAN called me and told me of his idea to create a fund for people with disabilities. I remember saying, "I have a savings plan for my daughter's university…why can't I have a savings plan for Nicholas' future?" Hundreds, if not thousands, of parents chimed in to a national conversation about financial tools that could transform the lives of people with disabilities from victims and consumers of tax dollars to contributing participants in our market economy and masters of their own destinies. The RDSP was announced in the Canadian federal budget of 2007, and our family has one now for Nicholas.

Previous to this plan, families had no tax-sheltered savings vehicle that could be used specifically for the future of a loved one with disabilities. Furthermore, if someone received government disability-pension benefits every month, they were not allowed to have more than $5,000 in assets. A friend whose daughter had recently turned eighteen was forced to sell back her daughter's prepaid funeral plan in order for her to qualify for disability-pension benefits — the funeral plan was worth more than $5,000. This "all government" or "all private" finance thinking ensured that people with disabilities were effectively poor and had limited choices in terms of their discretionary spending. The thinking was that anyone who had private finances, yet was in receipt of government benefits, was guilty of welfare fraud. To be disabled and accept financial assistance from the state meant you had to be poor, or at least be SEEN to be poor.

The RDSP, on the other hand, is a new savings plan that will assist families in planning for the long-term financial security of their relative with a disability. Over time, it is estimated that the RDSP will provide billions of dollars to supplement income, enable home ownership and enhance quality of life for as many as half a million Canadians with disabilities. The plan is similar to an education savings plan in that contributions remain tax-free until withdrawal. There are no annual limits on contributions, but there is a lifetime limit of $200,000, and these funds can be contributed by any family member or friend. There are no restrictions whatsoever on how the funds are used by the beneficiary, and when funds are withdrawn, they are taxed in the hands of the beneficiary at a much lower rate. For lower- and middle-income families, the federal government will contribute to the plan as well through the Canada Disability Savings Grant. For families with an income less than $77,664, the grant will contribute $3 for every $1 contributed on the first $500 and subsequently $2 for every dollar on the next $1,000. If the family income is over $77,664, the government will match dollar for dollar up to $1,000.

But those families with little or no capability to

contribute to the plan are not excluded. When annual income is less than $21,816, the Canada Disability Savings Bond will provide $1,000 per year without any contribution from the family at all. Currently, British Columbia, Newfoundland and Labrador, Saskatchewan, Manitoba, Yukon, Alberta, Nova Scotia, Northwest Territories and Ontario have all exempted the RDSP as an asset and income when determining eligibility for disability pension benefits. Quebec, New Brunswick and Prince Edward Island have exempted the RDSP as an asset, and have partially tax-exempted payments from the plan. Nunavut has not yet made a decision on the plan.

Of course, just having savings does not make someone happy or keep them safe. In fact, someone who has the combination of learning difficulties and ready cash is even more vulnerable to exploitation. Furthermore, someone who is in need of social care is likely to have very limited means of converting his funds into good living. This is where personal networks come into the picture of support. The PLAN values state clearly that people who have disabilities or are otherwise suffering from the effects of social exclusion need money AND caring friends to create a good life. Personal support networks consisting of family and friends who are coordinated in their caring tasks can fulfill a trustee role, ensuring accountability and transparency. The idea of distributive justice is difficult to apply when families who care for an aging parent or child with disabilities are so isolated. When my mother-in-law knew that we were struggling desperately with Nick's ill health, she used to say, "Now if there's anything I can do...but I'm sure there's nothing I can do." She was a kind person who was completely flummoxed by the scale of what might be required to be helpful. But when I asked for a banana loaf or company in Nicholas' hospital room, she was only too happy to oblige. The carving-up of a gigantic need into small, doable parts is the trick here. Ensuring that no one person is burdened by the lion's share of dependency work is key, alongside a shared and celebratory love for the person at the heart of the network.

Fiscal policies such as the RDSP that allow people to save without penalty, spend as they wish and participate in community life with the assistance of state-funded services constitute the elements that allow people with disabilities to convert financial assets to good living.

So, in Canada at least, families like mine finally have a financial tool to plan a decent future for their loved ones with a disability. Friends and extended family can help too. That's the good news. The bad news is that governments are scratching their heads wondering how to fund exploding social- and health-care budgets.

In Great Britain, politicians and academics alike are busy inventing new ways of injecting private funds into pension funds to pay for the looming long-term-care crisis. Young Britons are not saving given the current recession, which comes on the heels of a borrowing and spending frenzy over the previous decade.

In September 2009, I was invited to participate in a

roundtable of economists and accountants hosted by the Lord Mayor of London, Ian Luder. Professor Ian Mayhew of the Cass Business School reviewed the gloomy UK demographics and proposed a radical solution to funding seniors' care. He noted that although life expectancy is increasing (especially among females), we are not necessarily living healthier. Most people endure about ten years of infirmity at the end of their lives. Governments in all developed nations are considering raising the age of pension eligibility, if they haven't already done so. Australia has introduced a compulsory pension scheme and other countries are watching closely how that initiative plays out.

In Canada, health, social care and education are matters under provincial jurisdiction. My family experience has been in the Province of Ontario, but federal guidelines are such that in principle at least, there shouldn't be too much difference in standards of decent support across the country. In light of a proposed reinvented public/private partnership between government and families, what exactly should be the bottom-line expectation of provincial governments? I believe "adequacy" is the correct response here. Governments should ascertain what is required to support individuals' lower functioning. This should include mobility equipment, nursing services as currently identified for medically complex care, such as patients on ventilators, and of course residential care facilities for acute and long-term-care patients. The state has a duty to partner with families to provide and pay for these matters of basic living. But an important caveat here is that, if families are willing to pay for an "upgrade," they should be able to do so. Standards of care are nonnegotiable, but if someone has the means to provide French cuisine with a glass of champagne for dinner every night, they ought to be able to do so. Just because someone has a disability should not preclude them from enjoying the benefits of a market economy.

Higher-functioning activities, such as personal relationships, social outings, pursuing interests and offering civic contributions, should be enabled by friends and family on a private basis. But these activities do not come free, and often in cases like my own family, require armies of people to carry out. Similarly with the aged, we must find ways of including the less able into our community life in a way that will not bankrupt families and drive their primary caregivers to an early grave. Governments have a role in enabling active citizenship and rewarding altruism — secondary schools in Ontario are doing this by requiring community service from their students. Some corporations reward their employees who volunteer. The Institute for Canadian Citizenship embraces the value that "we believe that citizenship requires that one take responsibility for others."[43] Co-founders of that institute, Adrienne Clarkson and John Ralston Saul, told me that members of local citizenship committees befriend new Canadians and provide examples of civic contributions that are part and parcel of being a good Canadian. But contributions reap rewards and new citizens are given a Cultural Access Pass for one year's family admission to publicly funded cultural institutions. Currently, the scheme operates only in Toronto, but is set to expand to other regions across the country. This ethic of community giving and receiving is an example of a program that forges a connectedness between people that, if extended, will benefit vulnerable and isolated citizens as well.

Ethics and moral philosophy guides us in shaping the financial deal between families and the state. If we agree that it is morally wrong to coerce someone into giving care, as in my own experience or that of the Kelso or McKeague families, then we must accept that families have a state-supported exit clause. When families put up their hand to their health or social service department and say "I need help" or "I have had enough — I can't do this anymore," those civil servants should respond with practical solutions and no defensive, bureaucratic nonsense. Enabling families to contribute their own resources without fear of losing state resources would go some distance to achieving this ideal. Tax initiatives, such as income splitting for families where one parent cares full-time for someone in need, would be helpful.

If I had been able to claim half of Jim's income over the past twenty years, our tax rate would have been much lower. We would have had the extra cash to pay for more care and special equipment. As it was, on paper I could have been sitting home eating bonbons, because Canada Revenue did not link Nicholas' disability tax credit to my status as a non-"working" mother at home. My contributing role was not reflected in our taxation, so my contributions were not reciprocated in any way, shape or form by the state. Where citizens give care to others, policies must reflect an understanding that those two people — the carer and her charge — are linked in almost every way. The wellbeing of each is completely dependent on the other. Policies that support caregivers are essential to the health of their vulnerable charges, just as policies that support mothers result in healthy children.

Local community centres can play a vital role in supporting carers. At home in Ottawa between postings, I was an active member of my local community centre, Dovercourt. For a time, I was a board trustee representing the interests of those served by inclusive programs. Dovercourt is a terrific real-life example of how a sports and recreation centre can galvanize a community to embrace all of its citizens. The City of Ottawa partially funds operations of that centre, but participants also pay fees for programs. The centre's charitable status pays for free swims for people with disabilities, rehabilitation programming such as the rehab walking club and post-stroke aqua fitness classes. There are classes for all abilities, many for those with long-term conditions as well as for those who are recovering from surgery or illness. Charitable funds also pay for specially trained one-to-one helpers, otherwise volunteers help out. Secondary school students are encouraged to fulfill their voluntary-service hours requirement at Dovercourt. John Rapp, executive director at Dovercourt, once told me that the lounge with its Internet café and playstructure is "the living room of the neighbourhood." Everyone is welcome and after aerobics or aqua class is time for intergenerational coffee and conversation. The friendly banter is natural — differing abilities blend in seamlessly. Everyone is friendly with the residents of a local psychiatric group home who often come in for some company. When Nicholas and Natalie were small, I would leave them in the wonderful Kindercare facility, knowing they were safe and happy while I did aerobics in the adjoining gym. Family swims were a regular activity for us, but we took advantage of the disabled swim times if we wanted a quieter experience. These sociable and healthy pursuits made me feel connected to my neighbours. When I didn't come to class, people noticed, and prepared meals would often be dropped off at my door. All of these special kindnesses gave me a sense of connectedness to my community. It helped to make us all feel "normal." Dovercourt is a designated emergency shelter, so when the ice storm hit in 1998, many in our neighbourhood slept on cots in the gym. Although we had a hotel room, we used the warm facilities during the day to socialize and allow the children to play with their friends. This neighbourhood "living room" is just one example of interdependence realized and celebrated through public-private co-funding arrangements.

But it's not only seniors or people with disabilities and their families who benefit from such arrangements. Cristina Odone of the Centre for Policy Studies in London was interested in the aspirations and life goals of women in England. What she found surprised her and offended some. Odone's research showed that most women derive their greatest satisfaction by nurturing their loved ones.

Their careers are seen as an intrusive and rather unpleasant necessity. In "What Women Want...and How They Can Get It" (March 2009), she wrote: "Our work-centred culture is based on a fundamental conundrum: the economy depends on workers, while society depends on carers. Women, in particular, are torn. Only by resolving it will we create the conditions for a society in which adults fulfil their potential as professionals, partners and parents. ... Can — should — government intervene in such an intimate sphere? The answer is a resounding yes."[44] Odone's policy recommendations reflect her findings that women feel torn apart by a desire to care for their families, to have some paid work for life balance and financial security while experiencing the push by governments for them to be in full-time paid employment with children in daycare or face paying the penalty costs. If policy-makers were to accept my argument for the capability of enabling good mothers as a matter of justice, they might take up some of Odone's recommendations, such as:

- The government should change its childcare strategy. Pumping billions of taxpayers' money into a childcare system that is both unpopular with mothers and has been shown to harm children's emotional development makes no sense.
- Instead, through the tax credit system and childcare vouchers, the government should enable families to choose their childcare, including parental or close family care.

- The *Pensions Act 2007*, which introduces weekly national insurance credits for carers of children and the disabled as of April 2010, is a step in the right direction. The credits will count towards the State Basic and State Second Pensions. But the new proposals will only apply to those people who have twenty qualifying years of National Insurance (UEI) contributions...who reach State Pension age between April 2008 and April 2015. More should be done in this direction.

- The government should reform the tax and benefit system so that they no longer penalize stay-at-home women. Income splitting could redress this. Income splitting regards the household rather than the individual as the basic economic unit. It allows married and cohabiting couples with children to be taxed jointly rather than as individuals.

- It should be easier, not more difficult, for businesses to employ part-time workers. At present only a little over half (66 percent) of businesses have part-time workers; the volume and complexity of employment regulations are not likely to attract more businesses to take on more employees of any kind. The government should act quickly to cut these regulations and their accompanying paperwork.

- Finally, we need to break the stranglehold that a small coterie of women, who work full-time and buy into the macho way of life, enjoy on our public life. They have, for years, misrepresented real women who reject the masculine value system for one that rates caring above a career, and interdependence above independence.

Odone is talking here about the United Kingdom, but the policy ideas are relevant in any developed nation. She certainly seems unduly harsh to those women who have fought so long and hard for an equal place at the boardroom table, but I agree with her that the celebration of paid employment alongside derision for the work of caring is wrong and actually unhelpful to everyone. We all require care at some time in our lives. Indeed, a new trend to emerge (and this just from my own observations) is that of women beginning a new career path at age fiftysomething. Once childrearing is done, healthy and fit mothers jump into pursuing their dreams of becoming someone other than a mother. Many women find themselves at the top of their career game just as their husbands are on the point of retiring. I agree with Cristina Odone on most of her policy recommendations but I would warn her not to throw the baby out with the bathwater. Women do have more opportunities to succeed in business than ever before and we do not want to squander those advancements. But all of society needs to recognize that caring for dependants is not some dirty little secret to be denied or swept under the carpet. My daughter, Natalie, is at university and she has big plans for success in business AND a happy family — with lots of luxury holidays to boot. She wants it all, and I believe she should have it. Policies that allow women to nurture well with reasonable support followed by a retirement from caring should be available. Of course there will be some men and women who choose all or nothing on both sides of the work/care coin and why not? But where job satisfaction is concerned, Odone has echoed that essential PLAN value — that relationships are the key to a good life.

When it comes to our aging population in Canada, we have a lot of reasons to be worried. Many people still assume that the government will provide care and if state-funded services fail, charities will pick up the pieces. Tim Draimin, executive director of Toronto's Social Innovation Generation (SiG) coordinates the efforts to create a sustainable business plan for our country's charitable sector. SiG has been looking carefully at the UK model of enabling the development of social enterprise, loosely defined as a business with a social purpose. This is important for Canadians, because solutions to meet the housing and lifestyle needs of vulnerable citizens will be found somewhere between charity and for-profit business models. Enabling innovation in this area by creating legal frameworks to allow private venture-capital investment into charitable enterprises is the idea. The danger inherent in doing nothing to innovate is that numbers of people with care needs will grow as government budgets shrink. Families, especially women, will be caught in the middle. Economies will suffer, but so will people, especially the elderly.

One clear and present obstacle to assisting families in seeing to their loved ones' care needs is the fact that government budgets are strictly attached to services, not to people. For example, when I appealed for help at home, I was told that Nicholas was entitled to a long-term-care placement, but I could not use that funding if I chose to look after him at home. We experienced constant battles between government departments, each of which pointed to the other saying, "[I]t's not within our mandate to fund your family. Try another government department." In our case, that discussion most often heated up between the departments of health and social services, but it could equally have occurred between different budget representatives within a single department. A freeing-up of budgets so that they follow a person, rather than the services they use could go a long way to making life much easier for society's most vulnerable citizens.

A look at almost every tragic case of exhausted parents abandoning their children with severe disabilities, or even doing them harm, shows that the tipping point of despair arrives about the time of the child's fourteenth birthday. Some parents manage to last longer, but this early adolescent period is a wakeup call for mums and dads who believed that perhaps things would get better with age. The spectre of the endlessness of care demands for someone who is suddenly growing a beard or breasts can hit hard. The case of six-year-old Ashley X was one that caught the world's attention and triggered an ethical firestorm in Seattle, Washington. In 2004, doctors at the Seattle Children's Hospital performed a hysterectomy, removed Ashley's breast buds and gave her high-dose estrogen to retard growth and sexual maturation — a procedure that her parents say has kept Ashley a child. They maintain that it is easier to care for their daughter at home, to carry her and to keep her free from menstrual cramps. They call Ashley their "pillow child" because she is most comfortable lying on a pillow in the family home. The problem was that in May 2007, the Seattle Children's Hospital admitted that it broke the law by performing the procedure to prevent Ashley's maturation because there was no court order or medical review by a board of ethics at the hospital.

The problem with this treatment is that it is irrevocable. It denies the potential for growth and change in the human body — an extreme act that may ease the burden of care to families and state, but at a terrible human cost. There is no question that lifting, changing and bathing an adult is much more difficult than performing those tasks for a child. But a solution that is congruent with our most fundamental beliefs about dignity would not be the Ashley treatment. Rather, I believe that we should offer parents of severely disabled children a placement at the age of fifteen. If the parents choose to keep their child at home, they should be entitled to the equivalent care costs to be used in the family home. Currently, placements are virtually non-existent for those with severe disabilities who are not wards of the state. Most families struggle on quietly until their son or daughter turns eighteen at which point the relatively "rich" children's services become a thing of the past. Society hasn't woken up to the fact that this generation of children with severe disabilities raised in family homes are surviving into adulthood. Those with conditions such as Down syndrome were expected to expire in early adulthood only twenty years ago. Today, their life expectancy is within a normal range if there are no medical complications. In the parent groups that Jim and I frequent, the eighteenth birthday of your child is called "falling off the cliff." Some schools will keep teens with disabilities until the age of twenty-one, but after that there are often long waitlists for day programs, and a young adult is relegated to sitting at home watching television. Most parents have to give up work at this point to assume full-time caring responsibilities when their contemporaries are at their professional peak or planning an early retirement.

For parents in this position, housing solutions are often the most pressing need. Most want some kind of a home with the proper supports for their son or daughter, perhaps shared with a couple of other individuals who have similar care needs. Acccss to tax-sheltered savings such as the Disability Savings Plan combined with long-term-care funds released to the individual could go a long way to achieving this dream of "independent living." Innovative and flexible legal frameworks could give incentive to parents who wish to create a social enterprise in housing provision for their loved one. A house is purchased, refurbished with specialized features, rented out to residents with care costs rolled in and a small board of directors manages the household staff and payroll. Profits from rental fees go to repaying investors and paying for building improvements. Members of personal support networks represent residents on the board (if residents cannot represent themselves) and ensure quality control of all services. Residents use a combination of state long-term-care funds and personal savings (such as the RDSP) to pay for care and housing. All social aspects of daily living are arranged by residents or members of their personal support networks.

Seniors could use some aspects of this model. Most people at retirement age have some savings in a Registered Retirement Savings Plan (RRSP). I would propose that any funds redeemed from that plan and used to pay for care should not be taxed whatsoever. This would entail providing receipts for care received and submitting them with an income tax return. Any monies spent on care would be eligible for a 100 percent tax refund. Governments cannot have their cake and eat it too. Societies cannot euthanize all its citizens who are too old, ill or disabled to be productive and parents should not be allowed to surgically ensure their children never grow up. A new deal that incentivizes saving and allows private investment into businesses that demonstrate a social purpose is a way forward that offers some hope for a good life. Amartya Sen recognizes disability as a central challenge to justice. "Given what can be achieved through intelligent and humane intervention, it is amazing how inactive and smug most societies are about the prevalence of the unshared burden of disability. In feeding this inaction, conceptual conservatism plays a significant role. In particular, the concentration on income distribution as the principal guide to distributional fairness prevents an understanding of the predicament of disability and its moral and political implications for social analysis."[45]

I want a good life for my son and my elderly mother. But I also want a good life for myself. Some of the challenges that I have described in my family could be addressed by an injection of cash. But a life that we value and have reason to value is one that has at its heart caring and belonging. If life is a piechart, money is only one slice. The care of vulnerable citizens is a corporate act on the part of society; it's not just the job of social workers. It takes a village to raise a child, but it takes every citizen in every village to help sustain each other.

I have never met another parent of a son or daughter with disabilities who did not know what they needed to thrive. We know that paid care, together with the love and support of friends, family and neighbours, is for us the key to a good life. This is a future we must build for everyone, including those with differing abilities. For the sake of love and decency, we must be allowed to build it.

ACKNOWLEDGEMENTS

In the course of this book moving from idea to the printed page there have been many people who generously offered their expertise and encouragement.

First among equals is Dr. Susan Hodgett who introduced me to the Capability Approach and subsequently offered research materials as well as an "advice line" that was always open, and always helpful. Everyone from the Cambridge University Capability Network generously provided me with an idea bank, and special thanks go to Dr. Cristina Devecchi and Dr. Michael Watts.

Professor Amartya Sen could not have been more delightful company, or more generous in his support of my work. I will always be a great admirer of him, both personally and professionally. His introduction to Dr. Sabina Alkire offered me a new avenue of exploration that proved fascinating. I have Dr. Alkire to thank for enriching this book, through her assistance with Chapter 16, "Being Well," and enriching my home life through her wellbeing index for our family.

When I complained to Dr. Lorella Terzi that I had trouble holding on to complicated lines of reasoning in moral philosophy, she suggested that I go back to my sources and continue reading — a piece of advice that helped me to remain positive and hopeful, even when I felt out of my depth.

Eva Kittay and Al Etmanski were both early readers of the manuscript and their wise, critical comments challenged me to present my ideas in a more complex and truthful way.

To sustain my optimism, confidence and positive outlook, I have my women friends in London to thank (the "sisterhood"): Diana Saghi, Nora Lankes, Annie Maccoby, Beena Menon, Anita Ensor and Christine Fisher.

A very special debt of gratitude must be paid to my new publisher, Sarah MacLachlan at House of Anansi Press who gave my book its second life. Thanks also to Kim McArthur who initially published this book in 2010.

Without the loving support of our extended family, this book could never have been written. For their love and practical help, special thanks goes to Marjorie Higginson, the late Jean Wright, Karen Thomson and Frank Opolko, Cathie and Jerry Beauchamp and Rob and Carol Wright.

Finally, I am so grateful to have Jim, Nicholas and Natalie by my side. They fill my heart with love and optimism every day.

The Wright/Thomson Family Wellbeing Index: An Analysis

The author of the index to determine the wellbeing of our family is Dr. Sabina Alkire. Together with her colleague, James Foster, Dr. Alkire created the Gross National Happiness Index for the Kingdom of Bhutan (available at www.grossnationalhappiness.com/gnhIndex/intruductionGNH.aspx). The same "union" approach as is used in the Bhutanese index was used to analyze the results of our index — that is, all deprivations are counted from zero (rather than allowing some baseline of shortfalls from sufficiency to be present for everyone and yet they could still be evaluated as being entirely happy). We used the scale of 0–5, with 5 representing perfect happiness, or wellbeing. At the top end of the scale, Dr. Alkire and I agreed that a score of 4 was a reasonable "sufficiency cut-off" to be labelled as happy.

Anyone can replicate this survey. The essential thing is to choose three time periods and discuss with all the subjects the main events that shaped the family experience. Ensure that everyone agrees on definitions for the domains under consideration. Sabina Alkire suggested that I attempt to predict scores for my family members, which proved a fascinating and illuminating experience.

Overview

If happiness is "1" and unhappiness is "0," then each person and each indicator is weighted equally over time, this is what we see:

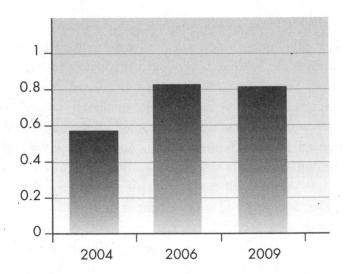

Individually Over Time

Seen individually over time, here is a line graph representation of how we assessed our own wellbeing in 2004, 2006 and 2009.

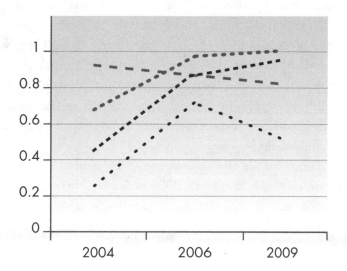

Looking more closely at individual results offers a deeper understanding of how we felt about the events of our lives in 2004, 2006 and 2009. The bar graphs that follow represent how much "unhappiness" was experienced by each family member in each domain that year.

In 2004, Nicholas and I had the highest proportions of unhappiness. Natalie had relatively high levels of unhappiness in the areas of friendship, community support, beauty and creativity and meaningful work. Her health was excellent, though, and she felt in harmony with nature. Jim experienced low levels of unhappiness in all domains.

Here, we see the unhappiness experienced by each member of the family in 2004. Clearly, Nicholas and Donna were the most unhappy family members, but we are able to see the source of their unhappiness.

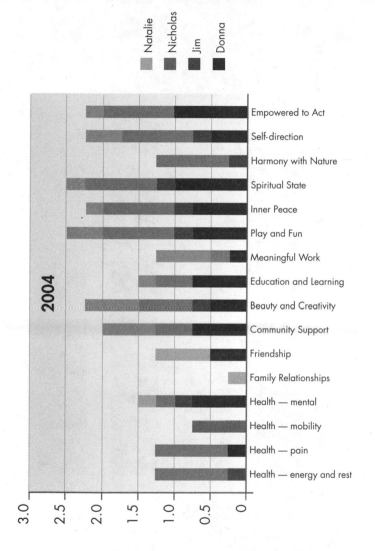

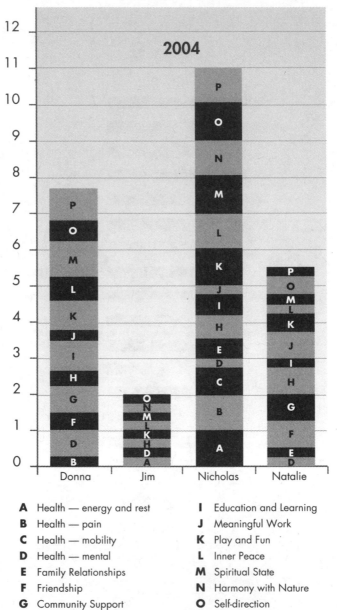

2004

A Health — energy and rest
B Health — pain
C Health — mobility
D Health — mental
E Family Relationships
F Friendship
G Community Support
H Beauty and Creativity
I Education and Learning
J Meaningful Work
K Play and Fun
L Inner Peace
M Spiritual State
N Harmony with Nature
O Self-direction
P Empowered to Act

The year 2006 sees an overall improvement in the wellbeing of the family, but Nicholas is still somewhat unhappy, especially in the areas of education, harmony

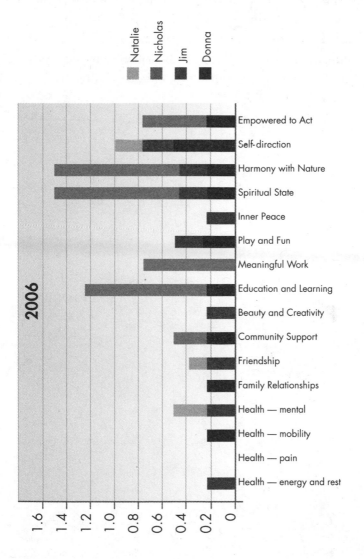

with nature and meaningful work. I suspect that his high unhappiness score in the area of spiritual state reflects his ambivalence about the domain itself. Natalie is very happy and Donna has improved significantly in all areas. Interestingly, Jim is less happy in 2006 than he was in 2004. During our conversations, he reported higher unhappiness scores in the areas of harmony with nature and general health and wellbeing due to the stress of a new job.

And note the differences in 2009.

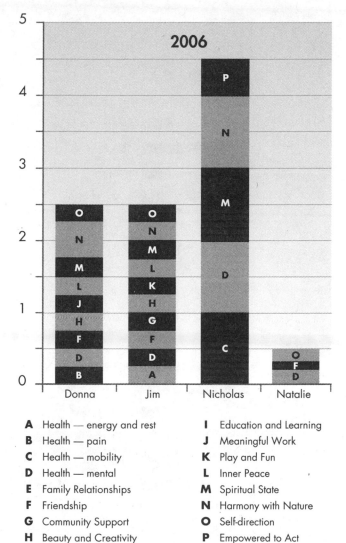

A Health — energy and rest

B Health — pain

C Health — mobility

D Health — mental

E Family Relationships

F Friendship

G Community Support

H Beauty and Creativity

I Education and Learning

J Meaningful Work

K Play and Fun

L Inner Peace

M Spiritual State

N Harmony with Nature

O Self-direction

P Empowered to Act

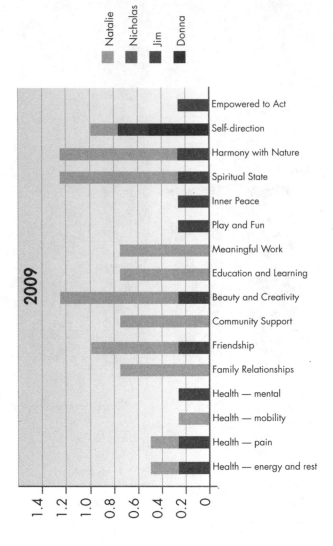

Natalie
Nicholas
Jim
Donna

2009

Empowered to Act
Self-direction
Harmony with Nature
Spiritual State
Inner Peace
Play and Fun
Meaningful Work
Education and Learning
Beauty and Creativity
Community Support
Friendship
Family Relationships
Health — mental
Health — mobility
Health — pain
Health — energy and rest

1.4 1.2 1.0 0.8 0.6 0.4 0.2 0

Natalie has scored a "4" or "5" in each domain, so she is considered perfectly "happy."

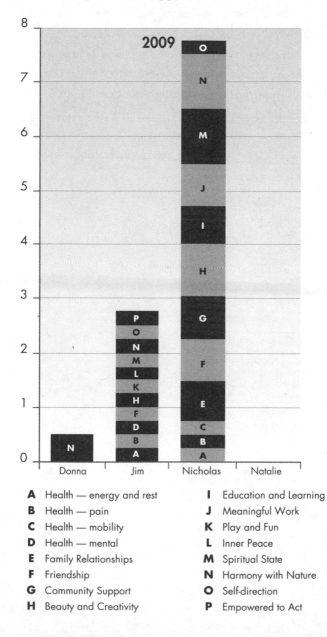

2009

A Health — energy and rest	**I** Education and Learning
B Health — pain	**J** Meaningful Work
C Health — mobility	**K** Play and Fun
D Health — mental	**L** Inner Peace
E Family Relationships	**M** Spiritual State
F Friendship	**N** Harmony with Nature
G Community Support	**O** Self-direction
H Beauty and Creativity	**P** Empowered to Act

As for Nicholas, it is interesting that he rates his health scores as fairly well. This is in spite of the fact that since 2006, he has become progressively more bedridden. Staying in bed gives Nick pain relief, but it causes him to be less satisfied in other areas of his life, such as self-direction, harmony with nature, beauty and creativity and meaningful work. Jim reported that although he loves life in London, he misses the extended family, weekends at the cottage and harmony with nature. Shortfalls in those areas cause his scores to reflect a slightly higher level of unhappiness than in 2004.

How Nicholas Communicates

Nicholas has a few spoken words that he uses to great advantage. He can say "yeah" and "no." A conversation might go like this:

"Nick, we are having some choices for dinner tonight. We're having chicken or beef. Do you want beef?"

Nick: "No"

"Oh, so you want chicken?"

Nick: "Yeah"

Nicholas can also say "video" (sounds like *veeyo*) and this can mean any piece of technology such as computer or television. "Video" can also mean media such as newspaper or magazine. He can say "Mum" and "Jim" (for Dad). He cannot say Natalie, but he will make a high-pitched vocal sound, like a girl. He uses that sound to refer to his sister or any other female. Nicholas can say "when" and he uses this vocalization to mean either "when," "why," "where" or "how."

He is good at developing codes for words that he is unable to pronounce. For example, Nicholas can click his tongue and we know that this means he would like to telephone someone. Because he is able to say "Jim," Nicholas refers to his best friend John Bilder as "JimJim." Nick expanded this word to include his Uncle John, so he is called "JimJim" also. Nicholas "counts" vocally by saying, "uh" (one) or "uh uh" (two). He will use this technique to discuss money, dates, game scores or PlayStation 3.

Additionally, Nicholas has a few hand gestures that he uses to great effect. His hand on his forehead could mean "Oh my gosh!" or "I forget." Sticking out his tongue means that he is referring to a competition and one of the teams will get beaten. For example, Nicholas will use this gesture in a conversation about the Stanley Cup or a PlayStation game.

When Nicholas was younger and able to sit in his wheelchair for longer periods, he would use a speaking computer called a Dynavox 3100 that he controlled with head switches. Nicholas would listen to word choices through headphones. He then clicked switches that were mounted on either side of his head to scan through these word choices and the selected word would be spoken by the computer. For writing purposes at school, the Dynavox could be connected to a laptop and the spoken word could be simultaneously written onto a word-processing program. The word choices are divided into categories relating to personal matters, people, places, things, actions and descriptions. Nicholas memorized many word scans in order to navigate through a large vocabulary, but he found the slow pace of the computer scanning frustrating and tiring with the head switches. Nevertheless, the spoken word, even one uttered in a digital voice, is a powerful reminder to the listener that Nicholas is a whole and compelling person. I always found it interesting that without the Dynavox, most people would speak to Nicholas through me. With the Dynavox, they spoke directly to him.

Nowadays, Nicholas is mostly limited to his bed, so the use of head switches is out of the question. All the scans, though, are written in a book and his helpers read the word choices. All the vocabulary is divided into two sections, arbitrarily called Red Side and Blue Side. A conversation would go something like this:

Helper:

Blue Side

Nick: "Yeah."

Helper reads the titles of word categories that are contained on the Blue Side:

- My Page
- Social
- Question
- Person/Animal
- Place
- Thing — Nick answers "yeah" to Thing

Helper: Scans the subcategories in the Thing section:

- Transportation
- Clothes
- Food — Nick answers "yeah" to Food

Helper: Scans the subcategories in the Food section:

- Fruit
- Vegetables
- Bread/Cereal/Pasta — Nick answers "yeah" to this category and more subcategories are scanned till he finally reaches his desired word, which is "bagel."

All of Nicholas' basic vocabulary for daily life is found in the scans that he has memorized. Any new vocabulary, for example for an online course, is added and reviewed as needed.

Communication Therapy Department

Cheyne Centre for Children with Cerebral Palsy
61 Cheyne Walk, Chelsea, London SW3 5LT

Telephone: 081 846 6488   Fax: 081 846 6577

COMMUNICATION SKILLS REPORT   12th Decemeber 1993

NICHOLAS WRIGHT   b. 30.8.88   age. 5.3 years
                       72 Northgate, Prince Albert Road
                       St. John's Wood, London NW8 7EH

Nicholas has now been attending the Cheyne Centre for advice on
developing communication skills since January 1993. As part of
this he has been receiving regular Non-Directive Communication
Therapy sessions (Special Times). Nicholas has an educational
placement at the Hornsey Centre where he follows a Conductive
Education programme.

In Special Times Nicholas has made excellent progress. He is no
longer a passive child who waits for adults to introduce
activities: he now has strong ideas about what he wants to play
with. These activities include looking at books, operating switch
toys, playing "house", dressing up with masks, telephoning family
members, and riding the see-saw. Nicholas initiates these choices
by looking for his communication book, then indicating (eye-
pointing and hand-pointing) one of six symbols.

Nicholas' usual accessing method is to visually scan the page and
locate the symbol he wants, put his head back and roll his eyes
upwards, attempt to point with his fingers, then re-direct his
eyes onto the page. Nicholas' extreme difficulty with eye
movements has become more obvious as he has tried to use eye-
pointing to giver specific messsges with symbols. I have no
doubts that the intention is there, but I sometimes have problems
interpreting Nicholas'' eye-pointing. It is important to check
that I have got the message he intended by saying "I think you're
pointing to the symbol for _____ " or "you want to play with
the _____ ?" _after_ he has tried to indicate his choice
through symbols. In this situation Nicholas' yes / no responses
are reliable.

It often seems quicker and easier for adults to communicate with
children who have limited speech through yes / no questions.
Nicholas still has a tendency to answer "yeah" to all questions,
particularly if he is over-excited or, conversely, if he is
uninterested. Nicholas has been placed in this responding role
for much of his early development but he is now becoming more
active and making the most of opportunities where he is given
periods of free choice with an adult present to facilitate play.

Nicholas needs time to use his communication book. Nick has
extreme difficulty co-ordinating listening and looking. When
being spoken to Nicholas almost always puts his head back and his

eyes roll upwards. The speaker then needs to wait for Nick to bring his head forwards and focus his eyes on his book / activity / toy.

Nicholas' communication book has 6 brightly-coloured Picture Communication Symbols per page. He uses an index to select a topic of conversation eg. people, school, home, play, places, food and drink. Nicholas has grasped the concept of using an index very quickly. He also copes with additions and changes to his symbols. He can recognise and use symbols after being told what they mean only once. Nicholas initiates use of his book within certain situations eg. Special Times, conversations at home, to give news, select topics of conversation, dictate letters to his family abroad, make choices and direct play. Nicholas does not yet have a way of asking for his book outside those situations.

Nicholas' progress within Special Times has generalised to home. He is now more active, and consequently more demanding. This has changed the family dynamics at home with Nicholas asserting himself, insisting on directing activities, saying "no" etc. Despite these difficulties Nicholas' parents have remained committed to this work as they understand the importance of this "anarchic" phase in establishing communicative independence. Nicholas' parents have also been working hard to change their own style of interaction with Nicholas, encouraging him to take more responsibility for communication and rely less on them generating ideas.

Future Directions

1.   Nicholas' parents are currently looking at future school placements. I shall continue to advise them on Nicholas' communication needs. He is making good progress with his symbol system and this will need to play a major part in his education if he is to achieve his potential. His future school must be prepared to incorporate symbols into the classroom and provide opportunities for Nicholas to direct conversations and play. Nicholas is presently in the early stages of expressive communication. His skills are not yet consistent; they are highly dependent on context and the skills of the adults working with Nicholas, and this should be taken into account when looking at future placement.

2.   Nicholas will also require access to technology. The focus of sessions over recent months has been the development of an effective low-tech system of communication. Over the next few months Nicholas' technology needs will be addressed. Nicholas has been working on the 2 separate skills of using symbols and accessing computers via switches. As he become more proficient in both of these areas he will be able to

integrate his skills and he can move towards using a high-tech communication aid with speech output. Nicholas also needs a powered wheelchair in order to move around independently. A recent assessment at the Cheyne Centre revealed Nicholas' potential for driving a wheelchair using 4 switches after a period of training.

If Nicholas is placed in a school where staff are not already conversant with communication through symbols and technology the Cheyne Centre may be able to offer advice / training in this area.

3. Another pressing need to address is the question of Nicholas' level of understanding. Nicholas' eye-pointing is becoming more reliable, making formal assessment more possible, although I still feel he has some way to go before he will be able to show his full capabilities. Working on expressive communication skills often results in children being more able to demonstrate their understanding. Although I feel Nicholas has some degree of learning difficulty I would be extremely reluctant to commit myself to estimating Nicholas' true level of understanding at this stage, as I would with any child with such complex physical and visual disabilities who is only just beginning to express himself.

4. Nicholas' communication book will continue to need expanding and re-organising in order to meet his needs.

5. I will continue to liaise with the Hornsey Centre. Although the Hornsey Centre and the Cheyne Centre base their programmes on very different philosophies it is important to try to establish a communication programme which can be incorporated throughout Nicholas' daily routines.

Helen Cockerill

Helen Cockerill
Communication Therapist

cc. parents
     Dr Cavanagh
     Maureen Lilley, Director Hornsey Centre
     GP
     Dr Diane Smyth, St Mary's, Paddington
     Carol Greenway, Educational Psychologist, Westminster
          Psychological Service
     Pamela Japtha, Special Needs Officer, Education & Leisure
          Dept. City of Westminster

News Articles

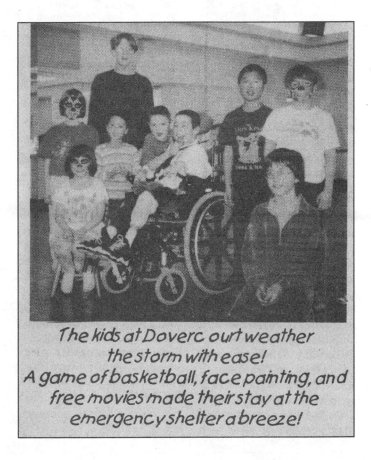

The kids at Dover court weather the storm with ease!
A game of basketball, face painting, and free movies made their stay at the emergency shelter a breeze!

The Special Needs Child in Hospital

special needs

Cascade
June
1996

In this article based on her correspondence with the hospital, parent Donna Thomson calls for greater awareness of, and training on the inpatient care needs of children with disabilities. As a result of her own experiences, she has produced positive suggestions for improved care, including a special needs form to help families communicate their child's individual needs to all the staff involved in their care.

Nicholas in hospital

My seven year old son is severely disabled with cerebral palsy and requires total care. He was recently discharged from hospital after a long stay due to post-operative complications following orthopaedic surgery.

Following my son's first admission to the ward in 1992, I wrote the chairman of the hospital a highly complimentary letter on the quality of paediatric nursing care of disabled children. Unfortunately in the light of our most recent experience, I feel that the situation has changed adversely and requires immediate attention. The dedication and professionalism of many of the staff remains one hundred per cent, but I also see many staff members who have been broken by the system.

I fully understand that health care cutbacks have meant that families of disabled children must carry a greater load of the caring responsibilities – however, I would suggest that nurses and doctors (both consultants and registrars) urgently require training in disability awareness and in what family-centred care means to those of us already doing total care at home and whose children require lengthy and frequent hospitalisations.

The ward used to be a happy and supportive place but it has turned stressful and gloomy. I know that I am not alone as a parent of a disabled child who feels that in such a pressured environment, I am somewhat of a pariah needing to apologize for the inconvenience of my child's special needs. Too often the cries of non-verbal and non-mobile children are not heard, or if they are,

they are simply considered a nuisance and acute symptoms are attributed to the disability in general. Furthermore my child and I seem to embody a pre-existing sense of failure and frustration in well-intentioned professionals; they cannot look us in the eye.

Problems with care

Areas of weakness in catering for the needs of families of disabled children include a basic lack of awareness. Staff are unfamiliar with the physical care and management needs of children with multiple disabilities and do not have the special skills required, for example, to feed children with oral-motor difficulties. They are unfamiliar with the philosophy of rehabilitation and base their care on the disability rather than the ability, leading staff to make negative assumptions about the child's quality of life. Nursing and allied health staff are often unable to communicate with non-verbal patients, and tend not to touch or speak to the child while performing care and treatment. There is a strong pressure on families to provide the total care for children who require it, and no opportunities for parental respite. In terms of provision for disabled children, there is a lack of appropriate adaptive equipment for toileting and bathing, as well as an inadequate number of disabled parking spaces. Every time the child goes back into hospital, there is a rigorous medical admission procedure with a continual need to repeat the child's medical history. There is then no flagging on the bedside chart about hearing or visual impairments, non-verbal and/or use of communication aids.

The concept of family centred care has come to mean 'parents do it yourself care' in this climate of cutbacks. Family centred care must mean something different for families of children with disabilities. Often an acute illness is the final straw for parents already doing total care. In such a scenario, returning home with a recovering disabled child who still requires nursing (often twenty-four hours) and is competing for attention with needy siblings is a recipe for parental depression and possibly even family breakdown – not healthy for anyone, especially the disabled child. The entire acute hospitalization process from intake to homecare must be planned and executed with the entire family's needs in the forefront. Parents of disabled children must feel safe leaving their children alone on the ward. At present we do not. I know that my son's acute medical needs will be attended to (provided the nurses are listening to his non-verbal cues). However, I know that his need for human contact, soothing, stimulation, laughter and comfort will probably be ignored – he is a good boy and I have taught him not to complain unless asked. All children need these aspects of healing – however the system assumes that young patients will fend for themselves when not being directly involved in treatment. Our children need special provision and protocols.

Training

I know that a system of training and awareness to facilitate better provision for young disabled inpatients can be achieved in a highly cost-effective manner, provided there is goodwill. We need improved education of allied health professionals on physical care needs, disability awareness and rehabilitation, greater accountability for quality of healthcare provided in hospital, and the establishment of a core group of professionals to establish a code of practice (including evaluation opportunities for parents.) I would also like to see :

■ the implementation of a streamlined admission procedure including pre-planning (for planned admissions) and a checklist for staff to gain easy access to information about the child's special needs, abilities and communication skills.

■ the inclusion of parent advisors on the professional advisory team and/or the setting up of a parent advisory team to consult on evaluation of inpatient care and advise on an ongoing basis – this could be in conjunction with a larger organisation such as Action for Sick Children.

special needs

Cascade
June
1996

Form for Special Needs Children

I have developed an admission form for special needs children which I helped to put together at the Children's Hospital of Eastern Ontario in Canada. It is still in use there and is kept on the top of the child's notes. It has proved helpful in giving staff a glimpse of the disabled child both as a person and complex patient. This special needs form includes general information on the nature of the child's disability and a list of all health professionals involved in his or her care, including social worker and occupational therapist. There is then a lengthy section on the child's needs as an individual – a short extract is printed below:

Do you use a special way to administer medication to your child? Please describe.

(First time in hospital)
Please list some behaviours that you know your child exhibits when experiencing pain (eg facial expressions, body gestures etc).

(Been in hospital before)
In your experience, can you list some specific behaviours/activities that you have associated with feelings of pain, as expressed by your child, in previous hospitalisations? (Please list observable behaviours).

How do you position your child in bed to make him/her comfortable?

Is there a special toy or blanket that your child takes to bed with him/her?

What is your child's usual bedtime routine (awakes at, naps, bedtime, preferred sleeping position)?

List some activities that your child enjoys (eg music/TV/stories).

There is also a space provided for a photo of your child when well and healthy. This is helpful in avoiding the negative assumptions that staff can make about a child's quality of life outside hospital.

Nicholas at home with his mother, Christmas 1995

11

Community

A child teaches the value of Friendship

by Donna Thomson, Mother of Nicholas Wright

My son, Nicholas Wright, has been a good friend to Eleni Wener ever since the two met in grade 4 at Churchill Alternative Public School. Eleni never minded that Nicholas cannot speak without a computer or that he used a wheelchair to play soccer-baseball at recess. Eleni simply shared Nick's addiction to sports, computer games and junk food.

The two friends have enjoyed outings to the mall, sports events and most of all, Nick has been Eleni's biggest fan in her chosen sport of ringette. Nowadays, Eleni and Nicholas don't see each other as much as they would like since each is attending a different school. But that hasn't stopped them caring deeply about their friendship. Last year when Rabbi Steven Garten of Temple Israel began preparing Eleni for the Bat-Mitzvah, he spoke to her about charity and a life which included giving back to community. Rabbi Garten encourages all his Bar-Mitzvah and Bat-Mitzvah candidates to share a portion of their gift money with a cause of their choice.

Eleni's Mom, Lynn Orect-Wener, recounted to me her daughter's determination to give some of her funds to a charity that supported disabled children. Then Eleni read a letter to the editor in the *Ottawa Citizen* I wrote about how a new organization in our city, Lifetime Networks Ottawa, offers hope to families with a disabled family member. Eleni decided right then and there to offer the other portion of her gift money to Lifetime Networks.

Eleni Wener presents her donation for Lifetime Newworks Ottawa to Nicholas Wright as Mom, Donna Thomson (right) looks on.

But Rabbi Garten knows that the seeds of lifelong giving will not be planted by simply handing over a cheque. He requires the young men and women to give a presentation on the charity(s) of their choice and explain the ways in which the organisations serve important needs in our community. I don't know if Eleni realizes how profoundly we treasure her gift for LNO and her friendship with Nicholas. I can imagine though, what a challenge it was for her to explain the mission of Lifetime Networks while preparing for her big day and carrying on at school.

Lifetime Networks is hard to explain because it offers a safe and secure future for the family throughout a lifelong support network of friends. It is firmly rooted in the belief that our quality of life is determined by the quality of our loving and responsible friendships. It is the layer over and above paid assistance that is true, unwavering, respectful and loving. Of course as families, we form this circle of love and support for our children who are vulnerable, but what of their future after we are gone? Lifetime Networks Ottawa creates and maintains this circle of friends for the lifetime of the individual according to the wishes and dreams of the family. It may be difficult to imagine who would possible want to befriend someone like my son for his life, but just ask Eleni; she'll tell you how easy it can be!

If you would like to support Lifetime Newworks Ottawa in any way, please call 748-7162 or email lno@magma.ca. All donations over $10 will be tax receipted and network friends will be rewarded eternally.

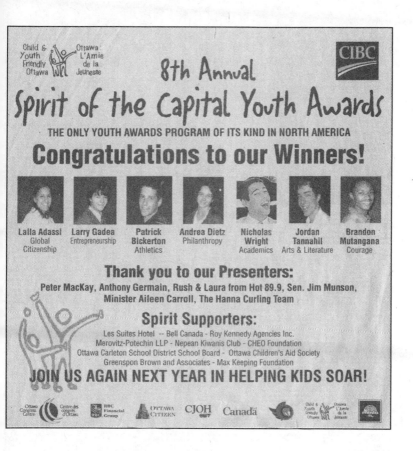

Society must not let parents lose hope

As the mother of a severely disabled son who is 12, I have followed the Latimer case with great interest. My son, Nicholas, has almost the same medical diagnosis as Tracy Latimer. He has suffered through similar surgeries and requires 24-hour care.

I feel deeply sorry for Robert Latimer and the surviving members of his family, yet my sympathy can be likened to that for an overwhelmed parent who abuses a colicky baby.

Any parent will know and understand the terrible thoughts and fantasies one entertains when a child is non-communicative and inconsolable. Yet my ability to relate to such parents evaporates when such fantasy translates into terrible action.

Robert Latimer and his family were victims of a tragic, complicated set of circumstances. The family clearly suffered from a dire lack of social, psychological and medical support. Mr. and Mrs. Latimer seemed to fear and abhor invasive corrective intervention such as surgery, feeding tubes and the like. Tracy's doctors seemed to have little appreciation of this when they advised the hip surgery.

My son has been hospitalized 51 times in his 12 years and has endured the same hip surgery, among many others. As a family, we have decided that Nicholas will have no more surgery. However, if pain became a big issue, we would ensure pain control measures were in place. Nick also has a feeding tube through which he receives medication and formula.

As his parent, I need to have a strong stomach, spirit and body to help my son cope with the bad days and rejoice in the good ones. The love, pride and delight I experience through parenting him has made me a stronger, more intelligent and more thoughtful person.

Considering my own family experience, and that of the Latimers, I wonder what can be learned from this. One parent, or one family, cannot care for a severely disabled child while sustaining a sense of hope for the future alone.

Since my son's birth, I have consistently fought hard for the supports I believed were required to sustain hope. My hope of future independence for me and my son led me to join the board of directors of Lifetime Networks Ottawa, an organization that seeks to form networks of committed volunteers to love, watch over and befriend disabled individuals as they grow up and away from their families.

Did Robert Latimer believe he could ever pass the torch of his love? I know he did not. The responsibility for preventing such tragedies lies with our communities. If society offers hope to families through support for less able members, it will inevitably bring strength and hope to the community itself.

Donna Thomson, Ottawa

Find new dreams

As the mother of a special needs child, I am saddened, but not surprised by the comments of those people writing to the *Citizen* in support of Robert Latimer.

I'm quite certain that few of the letter writers, if any, are parents of a special child. If that is the case, how can they feel qualified, let alone justified, in stating that he acted out of compassion for his daughter?

Taking care of a disabled child is difficult. Your dreams change as does your life. You must constantly watch over them, often help feed, dress, toilet and bathe them.

You constantly worry about them — but these are all things I do because I love my child. I've given up some of the dreams that we had as parents. I have found new ones. I've taken the sadness that came when my child became disabled, and turned it into strength and determination.

I need to help her in all her needs and teach her in all the ways that I can. I could no sooner think of murdering her [and let's not forget that is] exactly what Robert Latimer did] than I could a newborn or an elderly relative, who also needs to be fed, dressed, bathed and helped with toilet needs.

These people who are "horrified and shocked" at the Supreme Court's decision should probably spend time with children who have special needs. They should get to know them and their families. They should learn of the love that these children give so freely, the joy they bring to those upon whom they bestow a smile — filled with innocence and love.

They should realize the pride that most of us, as parents, take in these children, especially when they accomplish something that even their doctors felt they would never achieve.

These people should look at their own children. Heaven forbid that it should happen, but they should think of how they would react should their child suddenly become disabled through disease or accident.

For those who think they would act as Robert Latimer did, perhaps they should ask themselves: Would they truly be acting out of compassion for their child or out of selfishness in their own inability to face a future caring for someone whom they now believe is a burden?

Maria Portt, Dunrobin

Life missed

Regarding Graeme Hunter's opinion article ("Our two pictures of life," Jan. 19), our family also has a Tracey (our spelling). She is 24 and has cerebral palsy and many other handicaps. Tracey spends her life in a wheelchair in her own little world, she requires aid for every physical activity.

As her grandmother, I told my son and his wife that I understand how hard it has been for them and how much they had to sacrifice.

My son replied, "We are not sorry for ourselves; we are sorry for the life Tracey has missed."

Mr. Hunter, don't blame God for the "handicap" I am sure for many it tests one's belief if there is a God.

Tina Cutler Williams, Ottawa

Done with love

I have a handicapped nephew and take an active role in his life. This letter is my family's point of view.

Robert Latimer's actions were not taken because his daughter was handicapped but to alleviate her suffering.

Graeme Hunter's article suggests that a parent who would end the life of a brain-damaged, suffering and tormented child can be compared to a parent ending the life of one who "would never win a beauty contest." On the same page, Mark Pickup asks: "Would the majority of Canadians support his right to kill one of his healthy children?" Of course not.

Equality for the disabled and lack of physical beauty are not the issues in this case. Pain and suffering are. This seems to have been forgotten in the rhetoric.

I pray that if I am ever in an accident that leaves me with the mental capacity of a four-month-old, having five to six painful seizures a day and a feeding tube in my stomach, that someone loves me enough to put me in a car with a hose through the window and turn on the engine.

Linda M. Mundy, Ottawa

More compassion

I am absolutely appalled by the malicious glee expressed by those who propose to speak for the disabled after the Supreme Court verdict.

Having a disabled son, I am well aware of the fact that Mark Pickup ("The disabled must be equal," Jan. 19) by no means speaks for all the disabled.

I have had the privilege of knowing several people with severe handicaps and found them to have a highly developed sense of compassion for others, precisely because of their own experience. Obviously, this is not always the case.

Compassion cannot be limited only to those with a physical or mental disability. It must also be extended to those like Mr. Latimer who experienced psychological agony from watching someone they love slowly and very painfully dying while they could do nothing to help.

This was obviously understood by both the judge and the jury at Mr. Latimer's second trial. They had the facts before them and no hidden agenda. The sentence of one-year in prison and one-year house arrest was a very just and reasonable. It should stand. Justice, if not the law, would be served.

It's time for Mr. Pickup and those who agree with him show that they are capable of a little more compassion and a little less self-righteous grandstanding.

They might then come closer to truly speaking for the disabled community.

Deitry Zollmann, Pakenham

After experiencing the trials and tribulations of caring for her disabled son Nicholas, Donna Thomson is fighting for community support to help other parents in times of need.

ROD MACIVOR, THE OTTAWA CITIZEN

LETTER

The mother of all mud

Saddam's surprise for U.S. invaders. **B7**

Stay th

Charles Gordon's

HOCKEY IN CANADA

We can't lose our team

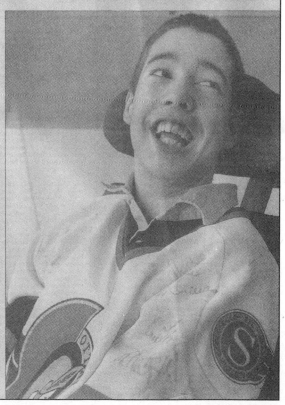

All this talk that the Ottawa Senators hockey team may have to move away makes me worry.

While I am only 14 years old, I have been a big Senators fan for many years, not just because they are a great team, but because they give so much to the Ottawa community, including the Children's Hospital of Eastern Ontario.

Every time I go to a game, I have a great time. I arrive early, get a hot dog and settle down for a really exciting and fun evening. I never miss a game on TV or radio and I read about them daily in newspapers and on the Web site.

My room is filled with cool Senators gear and I even had my wheelchair seat covered in the team colours.

If my team moved away from Ottawa, I would be really sad. Not only would I miss seeing them in person, but I would miss cheering for them at home with my friends and family.

It is time for the Canadian government and people to protect our game and our heritage. No more NHL teams can go south.

Bravo for Rod Bryden and John Manley for trying. If I had to choose between the Senators and the Senate, it would be a no-brainer. Sell the Senate, save our Senators club.

Nicholas Wright, Ottawa

A great loss

I am tired of people writing letters bashing Rod Bryden. Mr. Bryden is a strong community leader and should receive the gratitude of Senators' fans. Contrary to what some people think, the Sena-

Ottawa Citizen, January 18, 2003

Nicholas Wright: To be all that you can be

By Joan Shouldice

At the age of three, Nicholas Wright is attending preschool. What's so interesting about that? Well, Nicholas is a child with disabilities and he is attending an integrated day school program at the Community Cooperative Nursery School on Withrow avenue in Nepean. Although that's still not in the neighborhood of his Tillbury Avenue home, it's a lot better for his mother, Donna Thomson. Up 'til now the only alternative has been driving him out to Orleans.

Nicholas is one of four disabled children attending the school in the mornings, but he is the only one considered to be in the "high need" category. Four other "low need" kids also attend the afternoon program.

What problems does Nicholas have? According to Donna, He is not mobile, he has little means of communication and no hand function. He is in a wheelchair and has a full-time teacher's aid.

When asked what she expects her son to be able to achieve through integration at the nursery school level, Donna says her primary goal is for him "to be able to start living in the mainstream." He's at an age when attitudes are laid down for life. The children at the nursery school accept him as he is. "They are very interested in him and that's healthy... So far he has experienced no prejudice form his peers. "She and her husband, Jim Wright, were worried that if Nicholas waited until the age of seven to be placed in an integrated program, other children would already have set ideas and would be less accepting of him.

For Nicholas, being in a regular school is just the ticket. He's learning to use a picture communication device, and you can tell by the brightness of his little face how much he will enjoy the stimulation of other children.

With disabilities similar to Christie Brown, the disabled man featured in the movie "My Left Foot", Nicholas' development is somewhat delayed, Donna admits. Because there are so many things he just can't experience he doesn't have any concept of them. Currently he is using the computer to help him understand verbs such as run and jump. Donna is confident about his intellect and hopes he will one day attend college, work, and be in charge of hiring his own attendants.

His full-time aid, Stephanie Boudreau also helps Nicholas at home. The Wrights are expecting another child in mid-January, and Donna says that lifting Nicholas is getting increasingly harder for her.

Donna, President of the Parent Preschool Advocacy Group says that the children in Nicholas' nursery school will be the employers of tomorrow. The early exposure they are getting now to children with disabilities, may make them more willing to hire disabled people later on.

cholas' care is funded by the Ministry of Community and Social Services. In her lobbying of politicians, Donna has received support from MPP Bob Chiarelli and others who have agreed to make inquiries into more help for therapy in the schools.

Donna says some parents of

disabled children are worried that special schools are being closed down in favour of integrated programs, before regular schools are able to handle the special needs of some of these kids. A special program at J. H. Putman, similar to the one Nicholas attended last year, has now been closed.

Donna Thomson with her son Nicholas Wright in the costume he chose from a pattern book.

ENDNOTES

1 See http://nobelprize.org/nobel_prizes/economics/ laureates/1998/sen-autobio.html.

2 Keynote speech, Second International Disability Conference, World Bank, 30 November–1 December 2004. See www.worldbank.org.

3 Eva Feder Kittay, *Love's Labor: Essays on Women, Equality and Dependency* (New York and London: Routledge, 1998), p. 132.

4 John Maynard Keynes, *The General Theory of Employment, Interest and Money* (New Delhi: Atlantic, 2006), p. 351.

5 Written by Warren Nilsson for PLAN.

6 See www.statcan.gc.ca/pub/82-625-x/2010002/ article/11271-eng.htm.

7 John Restakis, "Co-op Elder Care in Canada," British Columbia Co-operative Association, May 2008. See www.coopscanada.coop.

8 Caroline Davies, "Martin Amis in New Row Over Euthanasia Booths," Guardian.co.uk, January 24, 2010. Copyright Guardian News & Media 2010.

9 Shoshana Zuboff, "Our Health-Care System Needs a Bypass," *Bloomberg Businessweek*, January 16, 2009. See www.businessweek.com.

10 David A. Pailin, *A Gentle Touch: From a Theology of*

Handicap to a Theology of Human Being (London: SPCK–The Society for Promoting Christian Knowledge, 1992), p. 103. Used by permission of SPCK.

11 *Ibid.* Pailin writes: "It is grounded not in what they (people with severe cognitive disabilities) can do or give, but in what they can be given. Worth is not a quality that belongs to a persona in herself or himself; it is a matter of a relationship with another person. …Worth is something that is bestowed by being loved, being wanted, being respected and being cherished. It is not a quality that is inherent in an object or a person: it is a quality that is given to an object or a person by another."

12 Hans Reinders, *Receiving the Gift of Friendship: Profound Disability, Theological Anthropology, and Ethics* (Grand Rapids, MI: Wm. B. Eerdmans, 2008), p. 162.

13 Jeff McMahan, *The Ethics of Killing: Problems at the Margins of Life, Oxford Ethics Series* (Oxford: Oxford University Press, 2002).

14 Eva Feder Kittay, "The Personal Is Philosophical Is Political: A Philosopher and Mother of a Cognitively Disabled Person Sends Notes from the Battlefield," *Metaphilosophy*, 40.3–4 (2009): 621–22.

15 Martha C. Nussbaum, *Frontiers of Justice: Disability, Nationality, Species Membership* (Cambridge, MA: The Belknap Press of Harvard University Press, 2006), pp. 77–78. Reprinted by permission of the publisher. Copyright © 2006 by President and Fellows of Harvard College.

16 *Ibid.*

17 *Ibid.*, p. 187.

18 Martha C. Nussbaum, "Equality, Dignity and Disability," in *Perspectives on Equality: The Second Seamus Heaney Lectures* (Dublin: Liffey Press, 2005), p. 110.

19 Theodore Zeldin, *An Intimate History of Humanity* (London: Vintage, 1998), p. 68. Reprinted by permission of the The Random House Group Ltd.

20 Reinders, *Receiving the Gift of Friendship*, p. 136.

21 *Ibid.*, p. 137.

22 Emily Perl Kingsley's "Welcome to Holland" was written in 1987. Reprinted by permission of the author.

23 Kittay, *Love's Labor*, p. 568.

24 *Ibid.*, p. 110. Kittay has written extensively on her belief that any idea of "normal" as a yardstick for judging humanity will inevitably exclude people like her own daughter: "I believe that positing a norm of human functioning — any norm, you name it, where that norm is to serve as a basis for human dignity — will turn out to exclude certain people from the possibility of a truly human life, a life worthy of human dignity."

25 Lawrence Becker, "The Good of Agency," in *Americans with Disabilities: Exploring Implications of the Law for Individuals and Institutions*, ed. Leslie Pickering Francis and Anita Silvers (New York: Routledge, 2000), pp. 54–63.

26 "You'll Never Walk Alone" lyrics by Oscar Hammerstein II, from *Carousel*, music by Richard Rogers.

27 Rosalyn Benjamin Darling, "Parental Entrepreneurship: A Consumerist Response to Professional Dominance," *Journal of Social Issues*, 44.1 (1988): 150.

28 *Ibid.*

29 Kittay, *Love's Labor*, p. 154.

30 Andrew Jacobs, "Pennsylvania Couple Accused of Abandoning Disabled Son," *New York Times*, December 29, 1999. See www.nytimes.com.

31 André Morin, "Between a Rock and a Hard Place— Final Report," Ombudsman Ontario, May 2005. See www.ombudsman.on.ca.

32 Shelley Page, "Whose Child Is This?" *Ottawa Citizen*, February 7, 2009, p. B1. Used with permission.

33 *Ibid.*

34 Eva Feder Kittay, "When Caring Is Just and Justice Is Caring: Justice and Mental Retardation," *Public Culture*, 13.3 (2001): 565.

35 Kittay, *Love's Labor*, p. 132.

36 "Putting People First," UK Government, Department of Health, February 26, 2009. See www.cpa.org.uk.

37 "Putting People First — Without Putting Carers Second," Princess Royal Trust for Carers and Crossroads Caring for Carers, February 27, 2009. See http://static.carers.org.

38 Arlene Kaplan Daniels, "Invisible Work," *Social Problems*, 34:5 (December 1987): 403.

39 *Ibid.*, p. 409. Kaplan Daniels elaborates: "The aspect of these activities most difficult for everyone to conceptualize as work involves the warm and caring aspects of the construction and maintenance of interpersonal relations. In the commonsense view, these activities occur spontaneously. They are informal and unregulated — outside of bureaucratic rules and

obligations. These activities are what Arlie Hochschild (1979) calls the positive aspects of "emotion work." They involve the following behaviours: (1) attending carefully to how a setting affects others in it — through taking the role of the other and feeling some of the same feelings; (2) focusing attention through ruminating about the past and planning for the future; (3) assessing the reasonableness of preliminary judgments by checking over the behaviour of all respondents in an interaction — just as good hostesses do when they look for signs of how well people are enjoying a party, whether or not anyone feels ill at ease or left out; (4) creating a comfortable ambience through expressions of gaiety, warmth, sympathy, and cheerful, affectionate concern for or interest in another."

[40] Kittay, *Love's Labor,* pp. 179–80.

[41] See Appendix A for a detailed breakdown of our index results.

[42] Canadian Institute of Wellbeing/Measuring What Matters, May 9, 2010. See www.ciw.ca.

[43] Institute of Canadian Citizenship (ICC), May 9, 2010. See www.icc-icc.ca.

[44] Cristina Odone, "What Women Want and How They Can Get It," *Centre for Policy Studies.* Centre for Policy Studies, January 12, 2010. See www.cps.org.uk/cps_catalog/what%20women%20want.pdf.

[45] Amartya Sen, *The Idea of Justice* (London: Penguin, 2009), p. 260.

"A Place in Society." *The Economist*, Sept. 25, 2009.
http://www.Economist.com (accessed Jan. 12, 2010).

Axline, Virginia M. *Play Therapy*. Philadelphia, PA: Churchill
Livingstone, 1989.

"Belonging—Living Ties." http://www.appartenance-
belonging.org/ (accessed Jan. 12, 2010).

Berube, Michael. "Equality, Freedom and/or Justice for All:
A Response to Martha Nussbaum." *Metaphilosophy* 40.3–4
(2009): 352–65.

Boseley, Sarah. "Thousands of Dementia Sufferers Told They
Must Have Surgery to Gain Entry." *Guardian* [London]
Jan. 6, 2010, sec. Society: n.p. *Seniors World Chronicle*
(accessed Jan. 20, 2010).

Brewer, Nicola, and Baroness Jane Campbell. "EHRC—From
Safety Net to Springboard." Equality and Human Rights
Commission (UK). http://www.equalityhumanrights.com/
fairer-britain/care-and-support/from-safety-net-to-springboard/
(accessed Jan. 12, 2010).

Brindle, David. "Row Delays Green Paper on Care Funding for
Older and Disabled People." *Guardian* [London]
July 8, 2009, sec. Society: n.p. http://www.Guardian.co.uk
(accessed Jan. 13, 2010).

Burchardt, Tanya. "Capabilities and Disability: The Capabilities
Framework and the Social Model of Disability." *Disability
and Society* 19.7 (2004): 735–51.

"Canada Health Infoway: Paths to Better Health: Final Report."
Health Canada, Government of Canada.
http://www.hc-sc.gc.ca/hcs-sss/pubs/ehealth-esante/1999-
paths-voies-fin/index-eng.php (accessed Jan. 12, 2010).

"Carers.org." Princess Royal Trust for Carers.
http://www.carers.org/ (accessed Jan. 12, 2010).

Clark, David A. (ed.). "The Capability Approach." In *The Elgar
Companion to Development Studies (Elgar Original Reference)*,
32–45. London: Edward Elgar, 2007.

"Cognitive Disability: A Challenge to Moral Philosophy at Stony
Brook University." Stony Brook University, Stony Brook,
New York. http://www.stonybrook.edu/sb/cdconference/
(accessed Jan. 14, 2010).

Cotton, Ester. *Conductive Education and Cerebral Palsy*. London:
Scope, 1977.

Daniels, Arlene Kaplan. "Invisible Work." *Social Problems* 34.5
(1987): 403–15.

Darling, Rosalyn Benjamin. "Parental Entrepreneurship:
A Consumerist Response to Professional Dominance."
Journal of Social Issues 44.1 (1988): 141–58.

"Dovercourt Recreation Centre." http://www.dovercourt.org/
(accessed Jan. 12, 2010).

Etmanski, Al, Jack Collins and Vickie Cammack. *Safe and
Secure: Six Steps to Creating a Good Life for People with
Disabilities (RDSP ed.)*. Vancouver: Planned Lifetime
Advocacy Network, 2009.

Featherstone, Helen. *A Difference in the Family: Living with a
Disabled Child*. Boston: Penguin (Non-Classics), 1981.

Gall, Yvonne. "Part Two." *The Current*. CBC Radio.
Dec. 2, 2009.

"Home | Council of Canadians with Disabilities."
http://ccdonline.ca/en/ (accessed Jan. 12, 2010).

"Institute for Canadian Citizenship | Institut pour la
citoyenneté canadienne." http://www.icc-icc.ca/en/
(accessed Jan. 14, 2010).

Keynes, John Maynard. *The General Theory of Employment,
Interest, and Money.* London: Macmillan, 1964.

Kingsley, Emily Perl. "Welcome to Holland." 1987.

Kittay, Eva Feder. "Beyond Autonomy and Paternalism:
The Caring Transparent Self." In *Autonomy and Paternalism:
Reflections on the Theory and Practice of Health Care (Ethical
Perspectives Monograph Series)*, 23–68. Leuven, Belgium:
David Brown, 2007.

—. "Dependency, Difference, and Global Ethic of Longterm
Care." *Journal of Political Philosophy* 13.4 (2005): 443–69.

—. "Equality, Dignity and Disability." In *Perspectives on
Equality: The Second Seamus Heaney Lectures*, 93–119.
Dublin: Liffey Press, 2005.

—. "The Personal Is Philosophical Is Political: A Philosopher
and Mother of a Cognitively Disabled Person Sends Notes from
the Battlefield." *Metaphilosophy* 40.3–4 (2009): 606–27.

—. "When Caring Is Just and Justice Is Caring: Justice and
Mental Retardation." *Public Culture* 13.3 (2001): 557–79.

Leadbeater, Charles, Jamie Bartlett and Niamh Gallagher.
Making It Personal. London: Demos, 2008.

—. "State of Loneliness." *Guardian* [London] July 1, 2009,
sec. Society: 1–2.

Marshall, Andrew. "Wealthy US Couple Abandon Handicapped
Son, 10, at Hospital." *The Independent* [London] Dec. 3,
1999 (accessed Dec. 1, 2009).

McMahan, Jeff. *The Ethics of Killing: Problems at the Margins of Life (Oxford Ethics Series)*. New York: Oxford University Press, 2003.

Mitra, Sophie. "The Capability Approach and Disability." *Journal of Disability Policy Studies* 16.4 (2006): 236–47.

Nussbaum, Martha. "The Capabilities of People with Cognitive Disabilities." *Metaphilosophy* 40.3–4 (2009): 331–51.

—. *Frontiers of Justice: Disability, Nationality, Species Membership*. Cambridge, MA: Belknap Press of Harvard University Press, 2006.

"OACAS: Child Welfare: FAQs." http://www.oacas.org/childwelfare/faqs.htm (accessed Jan. 14, 2010).

Odone, Cristina. "What Women Want and How They Can Get It." *Centre for Policy Studies*. http://www.cps.org.uk/cps_catalog/what%20women%20want.pdf (accessed Jan. 12, 2010).

"Office of the Provincial Advocate for Children and Youth." Government of Ontario. http://provincialadvocate.on.ca/ (accessed Jan. 14, 2010).

Page, Shelley. "Whose Child Is This?" *Ottawa Citizen*, Feb. 7, 2009, sec. Saturday Observer: B1/Front.

Pailin, David A. *A Gentle Touch: From a Theology of Handicap to a Theology of Human Being*. London: SPCK Publishing, 1992.

Pilkington, Ed. "Population of Older People Set to Surpass Number of Children, Report Finds." *Guardian* [London] July 20, 2009, sec. World News: n.p. http://www.Guardian.co.uk (accessed Jan. 13, 2010).

"PLAN Institute for Caring Citizenship | cultivate innovation and thinking, foster belonging." http://www.planinstitute.ca (accessed Jan. 12, 2010).

"PLAN Networks." *Registered Disability Savings Plan.*
http://www.rdsp.com/ (accessed Jan. 14, 2010).

"Planned Lifetime Advocacy Network." http://www.plan.ca
(accessed Jan. 12, 2010).

Pothier, Diane, and Richard Devlin. *Critical Disability Theory:
Essays in Philosophy, Politics, Policy, and Law (Law and Society
Series).* Vancouver: UBC Press, 2006.

"Putting People First: A Shared Vision and Commitment to the
Transformation of Adult social care: Department of
Health—Publications." http://www.dh.gov.uk/en/
Publicationsandstatistics/Publications/PublicationsPolicy
Andguidance/DH_081118 (accessed Jan. 12, 2010).

Reinders, Hans S. *Receiving the Gift of Friendship: Profound
Disability, Theological Anthropology, and Ethics.* Grand
Rapids, MI: Wm. B. Eerdmans, 2008.

Samuels, Jane (ed.). *Removing Unfreedoms: Citizens as Agents of
Change in Urban Development.* London: Practical Action,
2006.

Sen, Amartya. *Development as Freedom.* London: Oxford
University Press, 2001.

—. "Disability and Justice." Keynote speech. Second
International Disability Conference, World Bank,
Washington, DC. Nov. 30, 2004. http://info.worldbank.org/
etools/bSPAN/PresentationView.asp?EID=667&PID=1355
(accessed Jan. 11, 2010).

—. "Equality of What?" Tanner Lecture on Human Values,
May 22, 1979. Stanford University, Stanford.

—. *The Idea of Justice.* Cambridge, MA: Belknap Press of
Harvard University Press, 2009.

—. "The Possibility of Social Choice." Nobel Lecture.
Nobel Prize. Dec. 8, 1998. Trinity College, Cambridge

Shields, Sandra, and David Campion. *The Company of Others:
Stories of Belonging*. Vancouver: Arsenal Pulp Press, 2006.

Smith, Dorothy E. *The Everyday World As Problematic:
A Feminist Sociology (Northeastern Series in Feminist Theory)*.
Boston: Northeastern University Press, 1989.

"Social Innovation Generation (SiG)." http://sigeneration.ca/
(accessed Jan. 12, 2010).

"SSAH Provincial Coalition." http://ssahcoalition.ca
(accessed Jan. 12, 2010).

Terzi, Lorella. "A Capability Perspective on Impairment,
Disability and Special Educational Needs: Towards Social
Justice in Education." *Theory and Research in Education* 3.2
(2005): 197–223.

—. "Beyond the Dilemma of Difference: The Capability
Aapproach on Disability and Special Educational Needs."
Journal of Philosophy of Education 39.3 (2005): 443–59.

—. "The Social Model of Disability: A Philosophical Critique."
Journal of Applied Philosophy 21.2 (2004): 141–57.

"The Belonging Initiative." http://www.nurturingbelonging.ca/
belong/ (accessed 12 Jan. 2010).

"Tyze Personal Networks." http://tyze.com/
(accessed Jan. 12, 2010).

Unterhalter, Elaine, and Melanie Walker. *Amartya Sen's
Capability Approach and Social Justice in Education*. New
York: Palgrave Macmillan, 2007.

Welch, Patricia. "Applying the Capabilities Approach in
Examining Disability, Poverty, and Gender." Lecture.

Sept. 9, 2002. Promoting Women's Capabilities: Examining Martha Nussbaum's Capabilities Approach. University of Cambridge. Von Hugel Institute, St. Edmund's College, Cambridge.

Wolff, Jonathan. "Cognitive Disability in a Society of Equals." *Metaphilosophy* 40.3–4 (2009): 402–15.

Work, Great Britain. Parliament. House of Commons and Pensions Committee. *Building a Society for All Ages (Cm.)*. London: Stationery Office Books, 2009.

Zeldin, Theodore. *Intimate History of Humanity*. New York: HarperCollins, 1994.

Where Are
We Now?

■ ■ ■

Moving Home:
A New Life for Our Family

From the moment our plane touched down in Ottawa on August 28, 2011, everything about our family life changed. After five years in London, we were back in Canada for good. We drove Nicholas in a wheelchair van straight from the airport to the Ottawa Rotary Home — a cozy residence where our boy would now live and receive nursing care 24/7.

Over the next two years, Jim would retire after thirty-six years of long hours and high stress in the diplomatic service to find a more balanced life of consulting work and leisure. Natalie would leave the University of Toronto, bound for graduate school at the University of Delaware. I would forge a new professional path of writing and teaching. And Nicholas would explore living independently. He would visit often, but he would never sleep in our family home again.

Planning for our move back to Canada began months in advance. Long conversations with airline officials, intricate scenario planning and complicated packing lists were slowly completed. I began to make initial enquiries about where Nick could live and receive the care he required in Ottawa. At first, no one had answers or even encouragement. My first cold call to a local social service agency did not go well. When I explained that we were a returning diplomatic family that could not support Nick without twenty-four-hour nursing care, I was told that we would have no help whatsoever upon our return home. Apparently, our only option was to languish on waiting lists. The care funding we had won in our four-year appeal process was no longer valid because it had been mandated by the Ministry of Children and Youth Services and Nicholas was now an adult. We needed to invent a care solution from scratch, and we needed to do it quickly. We had just over four months to create a long-term support plan for Nick, ideally one that would last his lifetime. In the end, we managed to do it because a number of factors aligned to put our family in the right place at the right time.

Champions across sectors who knew Nicholas' needs demonstrated vision, flexibility and leadership, and for that we will always be grateful. In a way, we were lucky that our family had already endured a lengthy and painful appeals procedure. We also benefitted from the fact that the UK government assessed Nicholas' needs as being primarily health related (as opposed to social). Individuals with a primary diagnosis of developmental or cognitive disability are locked into sole funding by the social services ministry in both Ontario and the UK, but Nick's complex health concerns had always made him a hot potato — he was tossed between health and social care, leaving him and the rest of our family without help while the bureaucrats wrangled. It was clear to us that in both Canada and the UK, the health ministries were more reliable funding sources for Nick's complex nursing needs. Furthermore, although it was clear to everyone that a primary diagnosis of developmental disability had never been part of Nick's profile, he fell into a large crack between the funding criteria of these two ministries. Nicholas' health care needs had actually increased over the five years we lived in London, and he now had several new diagnoses to add to his already lengthy medical CV.

Our plan was to approach Ontario health authorities first. Nicholas was known almost on a first-name basis by medical and social support staff working in Ottawa children's services. But the adult and children's bureaucracies are entirely separate. Local service providers on the adult side had never heard of Nicholas Wright. Families here say that when their child with disabilities turns eighteen, it's like they have fallen off a cliff. To make matters worse, a returning diplomatic family with a son like Nick was a complete anomaly to the system. At first, it was difficult for us to explain to front-line Ottawa social service workers that during our years of government service abroad, we had never stopped being tax-paying residents of Ontario. The reaction we received to our initial enquiries about what services might be available to support Nicholas upon our return ranged from chilly to mystified. They assumed we were newcomers to the province and, therefore, our place was at the bottom of waiting lists. I wondered if they believed we were even Canadian.

At the time of our move, Nicholas was a twenty-three-year-old man under adult services — someone everyone agreed required twenty-four-hour nursing care. We knew that Nick's needs could not be met in our family home with a patchwork of helpers — the maximum allowable levels of home nursing would barely make a dent in his daily regime. Jim and I simply did not have the youth or physical strength to take up the slack necessary to keep our son safe.

It was clear that we had to find a housing and care solution for Nick before we returned to Canada. Nick could not move into our family home, even temporarily — if he did, we would all end up in the same vortex of pain, desperate fatigue and frantic hopelessness that we experienced in 2004. Luckily, the provincial government recognized Nick as a candidate for health services *and* social services. A couple of other highly complex adults living in Ontario had secured funding from both the Ministry of Health and Long-Term Care and the Ministry of Community and Social Services, so these precedents made our path a little easier. When our only local long-term care hospital turned Nick down due to his need for awake bedside night nursing, the door opened for a creative community solution. With a funding agreement in place, the search began for a local partner, one that could provide a home with qualified staff to care for Nick. Gina St. Amour, CEO of the Ottawa Rotary Home and champion of families supporting a son or daughter with disabilities, was my first port of call. The Rotary Home had just opened the doors of a new respite facility with a wing for children and another for adults with disabilities. The children's wing had received provincial funding for its operations but the adult side sat vacant, with only enough charitable funds to run an occasional overnight respite program. When I explained to Gina that we had secured health and social services funding for Nick's care, but had yet to locate a housing partner, her eyes lit up. "We would love to offer Nick a new home," she said, smiling.

After tearful goodbyes to our High Commission extended family, and with housing secured for Nicholas, we finally made our move back to Canada. Nicholas was wan but full of smiles. The first few weeks here were fraught with annoyances. We were shocked when we found out that the pharmacy could not fill Nick's complicated prescription for his spinal cord pain pump. Although the Ontario Disability Support Program provides funding for most medicines, we were told that the pain pump medication, along with some other very expensive seizure medicines, was not covered without an appeal. Nick's doctors had to demonstrate that there were no alternatives to these time-tested remedies (which in time they were able to do). Nicholas' medications are now funded and his future is secure in that regard, at least for the time being.

The challenges of securing housing and care for Nick were nothing compared to learning to live without our young man in the next room. Jim and I worried constantly. A couple of months into our new life back in Canada, I posted this entry on my blog:

> Last night I lay awake from 2–5 a.m. again. My dreams were of giant snakes in the lake at our beloved cottage. Why do I feel surrounded by lurking threats? I had no idea how my boy living apart from us would penetrate my days and nights with worry. I know that everything we did was right for him and for us, but at a cellular level, my heart and soul are objecting. The problem is that I don't know if Nick is safe because I can't check on him in the next room.

Now, more than two years later, I do sleep through the night. We visit, Skype or phone Nicholas nearly every day. Jim and I take a month away from home in February to escape the cold, and we don't fret or long to hold our young man. Sometimes, Nick is too busy to chat or visit with us. He has a rich life, full of work, amusements and friendships.

In some ways, Nick is happier and busier here than he was in England, but it wasn't always so. With the promise of a ticket package to see his beloved Ottawa Senators play on home ice, Nick was initially excited about coming home and moving into "his own place." But the novelty soon wore off and he became somber and reflective. Eventually, Nicholas blurted out that he wanted to move back home. He tearfully admitted that living at the Rotary Home, away from us, was much tougher than he expected.

Everyone rallied to support our young man while he was feeling down, and Nicholas experienced a real turning point during our first Christmas back in Canada. Perhaps he had initially imagined that we would celebrate without him, but being firmly in the bosom of our family over the holidays afforded Nicholas a new level of confidence and freedom from worry of abandonment.

He now finds meaning and purpose by writing his hockey blog (http://www.thehockeyambassador.blogspot. ca), which has received well over seven thousand hits. He is also active on Twitter and Facebook. But Nick's favourite activity is managing an online fantasy hockey pool involving all the interested members of our extended family, along with a couple of close friends. Nick would like to work, so recently, he created a CV and nervously delivered it to the manager of his local community ice hockey arena, hoping to be hired for a part-time volunteer job. He is learning that perseverance is a requirement of securing any employment, even if it's voluntary. This particular dream is still a work in progress, but he's determined to succeed.

Nick's paid caregivers are also his friends, and they often hang out with him during their time off, especially if something special is planned. The fiancé of Nick's nursing manager visits biweekly to play PlayStation as a volunteer "gaming buddy." All of these activities create a rich life for Nicholas — one that he enjoys and values.

Jim has more time now to spend with Nicholas, as do my two brothers-in-law, Rob and Jerry. All three are recently retired and have spending time with Nick inked in on their "must do for fun" list. As for mobility, Jim and I, as well as Nick's residence, purchased wheelchair vans, so transportation to sports events or the movies is not a problem.

Nick's health has been surprisingly solid since we arrived back in Canada. His seizures have plagued him from time to time, but we currently have those more or less under control. His pain is well managed by his spinal cord pain pump, lots of time lying down in bed and oral morphine. But there are always a few hours in the afternoon when Nick can get up for a trip to the golf course, the mall or the hockey arena.

Almost two years to the day after we arrived in Canada from London, our family celebrated Nicholas' twenty-fifth birthday. It was a very special occasion for everyone who loves Nick. I wrote this on my blog:

> I don't know how many times we've nearly lost our Nicholas. Doctors told us in 2005 that he might only have two months to live — an in-patient examination of Nick's sleep patterns that year revealed a terrible increase in obstructive and central sleep apnea, something that is untreatable for Nicholas because of his combination of disabilities. The palliative care team welcomed us and we tried to keep Nick pain-free and happy as we worried every day and night.
>
> On our return from London, our GP told Jim candidly that when we left Ottawa in 2006, he never expected to see Nick again. He marvels at Nick's strength of character and at the power of love in our family.

Last week our son turned twenty-five years old and we cel-
ebrated at our local sports bar with the family (minus Natalie,
who is far away at graduate school) and a small group of best
friends. Near our table, a ticker-tape display of sport betting
odds rolled over the big screen and I thought about how Nick
has beaten his own odds — he surprised everyone with his
hunger for living.

So, Are We Happy?

Recently, I decided to check in with my family to see
how well we had all managed to cope with the changes
we experienced between 2011 and 2014. I used the
Happiness Index described in chapter 16. I found my
own scores were nearly identical to those in 2009. In
other words, I am very happy, but I did show a slight dip
in the areas of beauty/creativity and friendship. London
is unparalleled for sheer aesthetic stimulation, and I do
miss my dear London "sisterhood." A slight shortfall in
my scores relating to family relationships and mobility
reflect new responsibilities for my mother. My mom is
ninety-two and quite frail now, especially since surviving
three near fatal infections over the past year. She's still
feisty, but there's less bite to her bark these days. My sister
Karen and I tag team Mum's care, but we both worry we
aren't doing enough.

Jim's scores revealed gains in the areas of health and
family relationships. He is fit, relaxed and has relished
spending time with our family. For the first time in many

years, Jim feels that he has control over how he spends his time and makes his life choices.

Natalie's scores are high; she is tired, but happy. We were thrilled when Nat was awarded one of eight full scholarships to study American material culture at the Winterthur Museum/University of Delaware. She is immersed in her passion — discerning cultural meanings in objects, especially textiles.

I was most interested in knowing how Nicholas felt about living independently. I was surprised to find that almost all of his scores revealed higher levels of happiness than those from our London days. Most dramatic were the increased scores in the areas of meaningful work and family relationships. I asked Nick the questions I had been longing to ask since we moved back to Canada: "Are you happy living here at Rotary Home? Do Dad and I see you often enough or do we come too much? Do you feel safe?" Nick's answers were interesting. He said that living at Rotary was okay, but he wished that he could live in his own apartment or back at home with us. At the same time, though, he sighed; he said that he felt very safe and he understood that he would not be secure in his own place or with us. Nick said that he wished Jim and I would visit more often. I laughed and said, "Well, *that's* not happening! We're already here all the time!" We both chuckled, but I knew that I couldn't let this opportunity pass to nudge our lad a little bit further towards a confident interdependent relationship with us. Nick reported that he knew we loved him and that we would drop everything to come in a minute if he were ill or in a crisis.

Our return to Canada has brought one more interesting change — a closer relationship between Nick and Natalie. Brother and sister now regularly Skype, and any sibling rivalry or old resentments have vanished. Both are delighted with their new friendship and are proud of each other's achievements.

What has made us all very happy over the past couple of years is the community support that we have felt from our extended family, staff at the Ottawa Rotary Home and everyone who supports Nicholas. Without that community support, no one in our immediate family would enjoy good health, happiness or hope for the future. With that support, we've been able to enjoy the seasons of Canada, savour each other's company without the burden of dependency care, expand our garden and reclaim our health. In our family, we all feel that we have a good life, and we are very grateful.

Our Family Contributions

Our family contributes to Nicholas' wellbeing in many ways that do not relate to his basic health care. We ensure that he has the technology he needs to engage with the wider world, as well as the opportunities to pursue his interests outside of the Rotary Home. We buy him a season ticket mini-pack for his favourite hockey team, and we ensure that he has the support necessary for outings to movies, restaurants and shopping malls.

Over the past couple of years, we have worked hard to "future-proof" Nicholas, to ensure that he will continue to be safe and happy after we die. We contribute annually to Nicholas' Registered Disability Savings Plan and are in the process of rewriting our will to account for the children's adult status.

Jim and I maintain our responsibility for Nick's health care decisions and we work closely with the team at Rotary. We use Tyze Personal Networks to coordinate Nick's family and paid supports in one secure online platform. Nick's Tyze site houses information related to both Nick's needs and his daily social activities. The care that Nicholas receives ensures that he is healthy and happy. The love and support of our family ensures that he has a rich life — one that he values and has reason to value.

Our family has much to be grateful for — we are happy, healthy, and we have personal freedom to make choices. Perhaps I am the most amazed by our change of fortunes. For many years, I thought such blessings would never be for us. I thought they were only for people who were untouched by disability or serious illness. But the lessons I learned in the "four walls of my freedom" help me now to appreciate every day that is free of pain and illness. Helen Keller said, "A happy life consists not in the absence, but in the mastery of hardships." We're not masters of all our hardships yet, but we're working on it.

What's New in Caregiving

The way we care for each other is changing. Traditional government-funded "cradle to grave" care provision no longer exists in Canada or the UK. Able-bodied people are aging into disability, and those with disabilities are aging too. Everyone is living longer, but not necessarily better. Currently, almost one-third of all Canadian and American adults care for someone they love with a long-term health condition, disability or age-related needs. By 2061, over one-quarter of our population will be sixty-five or older.[1] Given the low fertility rates of baby boomers, it stands to reason that in the future, able and healthy seniors will form a significant portion of the caregiving community.

Making the future palatable for aging or infirm citizens and their caregivers will require humility, imagination and collaboration. Stakeholders agree that the need for

---

1   "Fact Sheet: Selected Caregiving Statistics," Family Caregiver Alliance, accessed October 15, 2013, http://www.caregiver.org/caregiver/jsp/content_node.jsp?nodeid=439; Statistics Canada, "Study: Caregivers in Canada, 2012," *The Daily*, September 10, 2013, accessed October 15, 2013, http://www.statcan.gc.ca/daily-quotidien/130910/dq130910a-eng.htm.

wholesale change in the funding and organization of community care is urgent. The good news is that social change designers in the caregiving movement are intensely and creatively engaged in finding solutions that will "future-proof" our society.

Some of the most successful models of enabling effective community care have been those that lay the groundwork for families and friends to look after one another with carefully coordinated support from professional service providers. Tools such as Tyze Personal Networks that bridge family (informal) care with professional (formal) care are capturing the interest of elected officials here and abroad. Elder Power, the Maine-based care coordination tool described in chapter 5 is another example of how contemporary social innovators are borrowing from social media to help healthy older people leverage their skills and talents with the objective of caring for their less-able neighbours. Today, the conversation of caregiving change leaders is peppered with terms like "co-created solutions," "social innovation," "social change labs," "deep-change scenario planning" and "solutions-based advocacy."

For family caregivers and their vulnerable charges, the future is a work in progress. Dr. Bruce Chernof is chair of the U.S. Commission on Long-Term Care, and in his findings he identifies the tendency to approach long-term care through a medical lens as a barrier to positive change. He notes that people do not spend their lives in hospitals or doctors' offices, but rather with families and loved ones in their communities. Dr. Chernof thinks that solutions to our contemporary care dilemmas cannot be found in the construction of more nursing homes: he strongly believes that more community-oriented care delivery is the way forward. But he doesn't stop there. He envisions a day when family caregivers are fully functioning members of the care team whose services would be documented in patient records.[2] Recognizing the caregiver role in the patient's chart would embed the critical role of family in the circle of care.

Al Etmanski and Vickie Cammack are caregiving change leaders in Canada whose innovative strategies are recognized internationally. They are the co-founders of PLAN (Planned Lifetime Advocacy Networks) and internationally renowned social change gurus. Etmanski identifies three key elements to transforming community care. He says solutions must be co-created across sectors and partners, be driven by solution-based advocacy (what *can* we do, rather than what *can't* be done), and that all models for change must include the full participation of friends, foes and strangers. Etmanski has read the tea leaves for caregiving in Canada. He echoes the thinking of Dr. Chernof and believes, "The reform of health and social care systems and institutions must place priority on supporting those who provide the bulk of care — families,

---

2   Richard Eisenberg and Gary Drevitch, "Long-Term Care Panel Chief Speaks About Looming Crisis," Next Avenue, October 3, 2013, accessed October 15, 2013, http://www.nextavenue.org/article/2013-09/long-term-care-panel-chief-speaks-about-looming-crisis.

friends, co-workers, network members, neighbours, and volunteers."[3] Caregiving is still considered by many to be "women's work." But the support groups that Al Etmanski describes are almost entirely gender-balanced. In Canada, men constitute 46 percent of all caregivers and that statistic is likely to grow as men and women increasingly share the responsibility of family care.[4] It will be interesting to see how male caregivers will influence future trends in social policy.

Vickie Cammack, also the founder and CEO of Tyze Personal Networks, believes that the reluctance of the medical community to recognize the contributions of informal caregivers is the greatest barrier to positive change in social care. Her research into the positive health outcomes of network-centred care demonstrates that in order to realize a sustainable plan for the future, the modus operandi of the medical community will have to become flexible and collaborative. The family caregiver as a core health care delivery agent is at the heart of her collaborative care design.

Governments and the private sector have roles to play in incentivizing and supporting caregivers throughout the country, but they cannot do it alone. Idea incubators throughout the Western world are establishing co-operative, innovative funding arrangements across sectors.

---

3 Al Etmanski, "Quote," email to Donna Thomson, September 29, 2013.

4 Maire Sinha, "Spotlight on Canadians: Results from the General Social Survey — Portrait of Caregivers, 2012," Statistics Canada, September 2013, accessed October 21, 2013, http://www.statcan.gc.ca/pub/89-652-x/89-652-x2013001-eng.pdf.

"Change labs" are the model for brainstorming how stakeholders can provide affordable care for those who need it. These labs convene creative thinkers who want to both design models that can be applied to various difficult social problems and to play a vital part in valuable social change. These strategic partnerships and funding models are conceptualized in the change lab and then tested in small community trials.

There is no single solution to our current and future caregiving challenges. Rather, innovators are looking at platforms for crowdsourcing ideas and for devising ways that government, business and the non-profit sector can work together to enable care in society. Crowdsourcing concept proposals, grand challenges and prizes for excellence in innovation are popular now with agents of social change. When A Place for Mom, a private U.S. senior living resource company, recently launched a Senior Care Innovation Scholarship, young economists and business scholars flocked to propose concepts for innovation. Social media offers a myriad of choices for the flow of problem solving and idea sharing amongst professionals and end users alike. Widespread public engagement with online caregiving sites results in a shift toward greater acceptance of giving and receiving care across society.

All of these social change-makers agree that a shared perception of abundance, as opposed to poverty in vulnerable communities, will lead to positive and sustainable development. John McKnight, co-director of the Asset-Based Community Development Institute has — for over thirty years — led the movement encouraging communities to combine resources in poverty-ridden neighbourhoods. McKnight is famous for knocking on the doors of homes and apartments to ask people: "What are your skills, talents and passions?" He collates the results of his interviews to create community asset maps. These treasure troves of neighbourhood resources can be mined by individuals who want to trade their skills, as well as by local governments seeking to leverage the talents of their constituents in the process of community development. McKnight's work has forged the architecture for new research by Sendhil Mullainathan and Eldar Shafir, authors of *Scarcity: Why Having Too Little Means So Much*, showing that both the reality and the mindset of poverty cause its victims to make poor personal decisions that serve to perpetuate scarcity, hopelessness and inaction; poverty itself keeps people poor. Their research shows that innovation and deep social change can only come when citizens problem solve from an assumption of abundance.

The trick to helping communities find their own answers to caring for their citizens is not in locating charismatic leaders, but in forming "leader-full" alliances of elected officials, bureaucrats, members of the medical community, caregivers and care receivers. Government resources should always cover those in need of acute care and the intensive nursing of long-term care patients. But the non-nursing care of an aging citizenry is a matter for all. John McKnight challenges us to think creatively about how to lead a good life, and to think beyond our own individual needs to create positive social change. Perhaps the looming urgency of sourcing assistance for a rapidly aging society will provoke us to co-create solutions involving all who wish to form a partnership of care. Our future wellbeing will depend on it.

DONNA THOMSON began her career as an actor, director and teacher. But in 1988, when her son Nicholas was born with severe disabilities, Donna embarked on her second career as a disability activist, author and consultant. She is married to James Wright, the former High Commissioner for Canada in the UK. Their previous postings have been in London, Washington, DC, and Moscow. Jim and Donna have two children and live in Ottawa, Canada.